Teresa Brayton

In an Irish Twilight

An anthology of her Poetry and Short Stories

Compiled by

Bernadette Gilligan

Introduction by

Olive Morrin

Teresa Brayton

In an Irish Twilight

An anthology of her Poetry and Short Stories

Published by

The Teresa Brayton Heritage Group 2002,
Kilcock,
Co. Kildare.

Reprinted: 2013

ISBN 0954108515

This project acknowledges the support of
Kildare County Council.

Printed by:
Naas Printing Ltd.
19 South Main Street, Naas, Co. Kildare.
Tel: 045 872092
email: naasprinting@gmail.com   web: www.naasprinting.ie

Poetry

Crocus time 1
Daffodils 2
Fishing 3
In an Irish twilight 4
In the Spring of the year 5
In wintry weather 6
The roadway of my heart 7
The robin redbreast 8
Some rainy twilight 9
A Spring memory 10
Spring 12
When the leaves begin to fall 13
Bonfire night in Ireland 14
Cappagh Hill 16
The boy from County Down 18
The Cuckoo's call 19
Hallow Eve colcannon 20
O, Isle of mine 22
The land where the fairies play 24
Glenashee 26
Joggin' into Naas 27
The little bare feet 29
The Old Bog Road 30
The old fireside 32
The old home latch 34
A little field 36
The old boreen 37
The old road home 38
Owney the fiddler 40
Takin'tay at Reillys 42
To a sod of turf 44
When I was leaving Ireland 45
Tom Moore 46

Poetry

What Ireland is 48
Castlebar 50
Derry 51
Kerry 52
Kildare 54
Limerick 56
Old County Clare 57
Munster 58
A song of Leitrim 60
When it rains in Donegal 61
Because He came 62
A Christmas Blessing 63
The Holy Night 64
Hunting the wren 65
A Little Boy 66
A New Year's resolve 67
Life 68
Rosary time 69
To Saint Joseph 70
A Saint Patrick's Day memory 71
St. Patrick's Day 72
Carraig an Aifrinn 74
If 75
The croppies grave 76
Casement 78
Ireland speaks 80
The lad who came home 82
Parnell 83
A belated wooing 84
A nature story 85
Jerry Connor's forge 86
Patsy Maguire 88
The racing of Finn McCool 90
A deoch an dorais 93

Short Stories

A day with Pádraig Pearse ,94
In the heart of the hills ,102
Daffodils ,107

ACKNOWLEDGEMENTS

This book is a response to a local need for the work of Teresa Brayton to be made more widely available. The poems and short stories included in this book only represent a selection of her work. For helping to bring this long overdue project to fruition we would like to acknowledge and thank the following: K.E.L.T. for sponsoring the project; The Local Studies Section, Kildare County Library and Arts for their invaluable support; to the artist Kevin Simms for his illustrations, to Evonne Gilligan for typing the manuscript and to Sr. Fionntan Dáibhís for proof reading. We would also like to acknowledge the wholehearted support of James McArdle our colleagues Breda Rogers, Seán Montague, Jim Rochfort and Mary Costello.

Front Cover: Background handwriting from a Teresa Brayton manuscript courtesy Kildare County Library and Arts

Inset on front cover: Teresa Brayton in her later years. Photo courtesy Kildare County Library and Arts.

Back Cover: The Old Bog Road
Photo: B. Gilligan

Dedicated to the memory of

Máirtín and Mícheál Cowley
Kilbrook

Introduction

Teresa Coca Brayton was born into a nationalist family in Kilbrook, Kilcock on 29th June 1868. Her father was Hugh Boylan and her mother Elizabeth Downes. The Boylans were prominent during the 1798 Rebellion, her great grandfather led a battalion of pikesmen at the Battle of Prosperous. Raised in such an atmosphere, she later used her talent and articulated her nationalist instinct during the Land League period by writing poetry which was published in The Nation, Young Ireland, Westmeath Independent and Kings County Chronicle under the pen-name of T.B. Kilbrook. She attended Newtown National School and became an assistant teacher to her sister Elizabeth. In later years she disclosed that she had won a literary award at the age of twelve.

In September 1895 Teresa Boylan emigrated to America. She settled first in Boston but then moved to New York where she met and married Richard Brayton a French-Canadian who worked in the Municipal Revenue Department. It was as Teresa Brayton that she became known as a writer of poetry. She became well known in Irish American circles and her poems appeared in The Irish World, New York, The San Francisco Monitor, The Syracuse Sun, The Rosary Magazine and many other publications. The Old Bog Road which was set to music by Mrs. Madeline King O'Farrelly a native of Rochfordbridge, Co. Westmeath, was included in her book of poetry called Songs of the Dawn. Teresa Brayton returned to Ireland a number of times and was personally acquainted with most of the leaders of the 1916 Rebellion. Her commitment to the struggle for Irish freedom was unstinting, and she used her pen unreservedly in highlighting and promoting the 'cause'. She engaged in fundraising and wrote poems in honour of several Irish patriots including Parnell, Casement and Pearse. An editorial at the time in the Catholic Columbian proposes that Teresa Brayton may well be hailed as the poet of the Irish Rebellion.

In recognition of her efforts Countess Markievicz sent a chip of the flagstaff which flew over the GPO during the 1916 Rising to Teresa Brayton as a tribute to your beautiful verses that are an inspiration to lovers of freedom and justice. She treasured this souvenir of the Rising until her death. This momento now resides with her other memorabilia in the Teresa Brayton Memorial Library, Kilcock, Co. Kildare.

She also had a practical view on how political stability would benefit economic progress. On one of her visits home to Ireland she was interviewed for the Mayo News which appeared on the 29th June 1912. When questioned on the high level of emigration at the time her response was A satisfactory settlement of the land question and re-possession of a native Parliament should not alone tend to stem the tide of emigration, but should also be powerful factors in drawing back the sea-divided Gaels to their motherland. With the foundations of national prosperity firmly set, I believe there will be no lack of foreign capital to start the wheels running again.

Unlike most exiles Teresa Brayton returned permanently to Ireland in 1932 aged sixty-four. She lived a further eleven years in Ireland first in Bray, later at North Strand, Dublin where she experienced the bombing of the North Strand during the Second World War. She spent the last three years of her life in Kilbrook and died in the room in which she was born on the 19th August 1943. She is buried in nearby Cloncurry graveyard.

William Walsh a close friend of Teresa Brayton's described her as *shy and reserved when in a crowded room. She was at home only with those who shared her interests but if one were interested in poetry or the arts she asked no more. She had a richly stored mind and was never less alone than when alone.* On his last visit to her in 1941 in Kilbrook he remembers *her bobbed silver hair framing a calm face, the most striking features of which were her bright alert blue eyes.*

In 1913 her first book of poetry was published in New York called the *Songs of the Dawn*. The *Flame of Ireland* appeared in 1926 and *Christmas Verses*, her only book published in Ireland came out in 1934. Other poems and short stories were published in newspapers and periodicals both in the United States and Ireland. The main themes, which permeate her poetry, are the exile's nostalgic loss of homeland, nationalism and religion. The emigrants' theme was often localised and personalised and many of her poems are enveloped by her love of nature and her keen awareness of the changing seasons. In an article about Teresa Brayton in the *Caupchin Annual* James Flynn claims the *the notable and distinguished thing about her writing is its close adherence to the old bardic traditions. Scarcely any other Anglo-Irish poet has recalled so vividly the old world of Gaeldom.*

As an admirer of Éamon de Valera she told an Irish Press reporter on her return to Ireland in 1932 *I feel that it is the crowning glory of my return to Ireland that Mr. De Valera's party has come to power. I think the answer to Pádraig Pearse's words 'What if my dream should come true?' is already taking place in Ireland today.*

At the instigation of Enfield Muintir na Tire, President de Valera as a tribute to Teresa Brayton agreed to unveil a memorial cross over her grave on the 18th October 1959. After the unveiling Rev. Seán Corkery, Librarian of St. Patrick's College, Maynooth proposed a vote of thanks to the President and said they were extremely grateful to him for performing the ceremony. On 8th September 2002 Fr. Paul O'Boyle, Curate of Kilcock and Newtown Parish unveiled a stone plaque in honour of Teresa Brayton in Newtown Community Centre where she went to school and taught as an assistant teacher. The inscription on the plaque comes from her poem 'When I was leaving Ireland' and probably encapsulates the essence of Teresa Brayton.

But I'll go back to Ireland in life or death I'll go

Crocus time

Last night I saw a meteor stream
Down God's o'ereaching blue,
And wistfully I dreamed a dream
Of crocus time and you;
For crocuses are amber tipped,
And amber haired were you,
And amber was the star that slipped
Down God's great arch of blue.

Above the hill of Innisgar
It swept aloft, alone,
But down the range of sun and star
Its utmost flight was known;
But O, my crocus, amber tipped,
Where shall I seek for you
When time for me his bonds have slipped
In God's eternal blue?

Daffodils

Grey skies, a sodden street and driving rain,
A loneliness that more than winter chills,
Then lo, behind a florist's window pane
The flash of daffodils.

Like chidden children stand they downcast there,
Weary and fading in an alien place,
While I - I see again my own Kildare,
Where winds of springtime race.

There on the breast of nature all astir
Young grasses shiver in the early morn,
There blossoms, tender as the soul of her
Whiten the damson thorn.

I hear a cuckoo, now anear, now far,
Chant his gay song along the freshening hills,
And in my father's garden, star by star,
Blossom the daffodils.

O lowering skies, grey rain and sodden street,
I see you not, for memory- led I turn
Back to a land where dawns are misty sweet,
And lingering twilights burn.

Where a wet spring wind, like the kiss of God,
Hedge guarded hollows with young violets fills,
And, curtseying across the greening sod,
Laugh Ireland's daffodils.

Fishing

One day in summer I went a fishing
Where Dublin reaches to meet Kildare,
And nobly laden beyond all wishing
The cool of the evening found me there.
The bells from Leixlip were softly falling
Across the meadows in vesper chime,
And the song of a sleepy thrush was calling
The world to rest with his silver rhyme.

You came down walking beside the river,
While corncrakes shrilled to the darkening skies,
And I the fisher, was caught forever
By the lure of love in your dreamy eyes.
The primrose blossoms were blooming round you,
The winds were kissing your braided hair,
Now the fish are safe since the day I found you
Where Dublin reaches to meet Kildare.

In an Irish twilight

I'm seeing nothing but a whitethorn tree,
I'm hearing nothing but a May wind's sigh,
Here at the dusky bedtime of the bee
Yet well I know 'tis not alone am I.

Sure little feet are dancing where I stand
And merry eyes salute me from the dew,
O, Gentle People of my motherland
I come back, weary of the world, to you.

In the Spring of the year

In the spring of the year we went walking,
O, but the greening meadows were sweet,
And God to His world of love was talking
    In every daisy above our feet.
My heart was singing with joy and laughter,
    O, soul of my bosom, if I but knew
The desolate days that were speeding after
    When I'd go walking no more with you.

In the spring of the year you lay dying
The greening meadows were wild with rain
And God to His world of woe was sighing
    In every splash on the window pane;
Drooping to rest like a sea beat swallow
    I felt you slipping away from me,
And the pitiful feet of me could not follow
    Beyond those shadows of mystery.

Now years keep coming and years keep going,
    Little I heed them green or grey,
Watching the river of life whose flowing
    Must sometime bring me a brighter day.
Then spring o'the year or depth of winter
    God will be talking of joy agin
To me and His world when I shall enter
    The same soft shadows where you went in.

In wintry weather

Once on a day of December weather,
Greyest and wildest of wintry days,
We, who once were children together,
Kissed and passed unto separate ways.
I returning to worldly duty
Sick with the grief that had crossed my years,
And you, with a smile of wondrous beauty
To the far off Country that knows no tears.

Following unto untravelled distance
The guiding touch of God's messenger,
Fearless you went in His strong assistance
Who called you home where His angels were.
And I, fearing lest your sleep's completeness
Be vaguely troubled by noisy woe,
Kissing your brow of unruffled sweetness
Passed out, sore hearted and left you so.

But oft when the sunset's gates at even
Shimmer all crimson and golden barred,
I think of you in that shining heaven
Whose floor is the firmament planet starred.
And out of my life's December weather
I pray you to guard my lonely years
Till we, who once were children together,
Will meet in the Country that knows no tears.

The roadway of my heart

A big road circles round the world, sure, fine it is they say,
But the little boreen of my heart runs lone and far away.
'Tis winding over weary seas with many a sigh beset,
But O, of all the roads I know it is the dearest yet.

By common ways and common graves and common homes it goes
But no one knows its beauty like the soul within me knows;
Its dawns are drenched with dews from heaven, its nights are tearful sweet,
And sometimes One long crucified walks there to guide my feet.

It leads me down by purple hills where fairies sport o' nights
It shows me many a hawthorn lane, the scene of dead delights,
It clothes again with living fire the faces laid away
Beneath the cold of grass and mould, my road of yesterday.

O, twilit boreen of my heart, the world is vague and vast
But you are holy with the balm of all my hallowed past;
You thrill me with the touch of hands my hands were wont to hold,
You lure me with the lilt of dreams I dreamed and lost of old.

The big road of the world leads on by many a stately town,
But the little boreen of my heart keeps ever drifting down
By common ways and common graves and common homes, but, oh!
Of all the roads in life it is the sweetest road I know.

The robin redbreast

The blackbird is a noble bird, and sings a noble note;
And sure, a flock of fiddles play in the brown thrush's throat;
The bandit cuckoo's song in spring is worth a King's command,
When hawthorn buds are blossoming and May is in the land;
But, over every bird that sings in air or thorn or sedge,
Give me the robin redbreast, in an Irish hedge.

You, who were born in Ireland, do you remember now
How he'd cock his head toward you across a garden bough,
When autumn's leaves were whirling down in clouds about you feet,
And they thatched the long potato pits and carried home the peat.
How his wistful song would follow you from wind swept bush to bush,
As you hurried home while turf smoke filled the evening's hush.

Och! youth is long behind me, and my hair is brown no more,
Tho' I've money in my pocket, and I own a thriving store;
But when the radiator sings its winter song of steam,
And myself is cocked beside it, I lean my head to dream
Of frosty evenings far away across the big world's edge,
And the robin redbreast singing, in an Irish hedge.

Some rainy twilight

Some rainy twilight when the elms are weeping
Soft little tears o'er spring's young growing things,
Before the first wee primroses are peeping
And no bird save the robin redbreast sings;
Some rainy twilight when the clouds, low-driven,
Cluster, like children by Knockmany's knee,
Lean out awhile beyond the sills of heaven
And send a whisper through the dusk to me.

Some rainy twilight when the homing swallows
Wing their low flight along the freshening hills,
And laughing April over hills and hollows
Blows out the torches of the daffodils;
Some rainy twilight when my spirit, shriven
And healed of sorrow, may draw close to thee,
Sweetheart, lean outbeyond the sills of heaven
And breathe a whisper in the dusk to me.

A Spring memory

Oh, it was in the pleasant spring weather,
When daffodils shone on the lea;
A new bloom was bright on the heather
And spring winds blew in from the sea;
A blackbird sweet music was making
Below in the blossoming dell,
And nature to gladness was waking
That day when we met at the well.

Your eyes were like Avon's brown water
When shaded by summer-clad trees,
Your voice like the blackbirds in Oughter,
Your step was as free as the breeze;
And I with my brimming pail lingered
To while the sweet moments away,
Till evening came in dewy fingered
And closed the dead eyelids of day.

We talked of the news and the weather,
And chatted of things round about;
How bright was the bloom of the heather,
How bravely the young leaves hung out;
And then in a whisper you told me
The story that ever is new,
And I with the stars to behold me
Repeated that love tale to you.

Alas for the days that are over!
Alas for the springs that are dead!
Alas for the dusky eyed lover
Who lies with the mould at his head!
And though a March wind there is blowing
And daffodils shine on the lea,
An ocean is foaming and flowing
Between my far country and me!

But in the dim palace of dreaming
My fancy sees visions by night
Of dewy eyes, dusky and gleaming
Like Avon's waves checkered by light;
And sun-like in rain darkened weather
This picture arises to me;
A youth and a maiden together
When spring winds blew in from the sea.

Spring

Shy as a village maiden down from the mountains tripping,
Pelted by tomboy winds that joy to play with a mate so fair,
Hiding here by a dripping hedge, there over sedges slipping,
Peering through misty veilings with a lilac plume in her hair.

Lured by a timid violet here, there by a robin's whistle,
Taunted by flaming daffodils that beckon the swallows wing,
Soft as a baby's hand at the breast, light as the lint of the thistle,
Over the rain of the wheeling world passes the angel, Spring.

When the leaves begin to fall

When the days are growing shorter and the nights are getting long
And there comes a sort of sadness in the robin's evening song
A feeling of contentment settles down upon us all
For our busy days are over when the leaves begin to fall.

When the hay is in the haggard and the oats are in the barn
And the women start their knitting rolling balls of woollen yarn
There's a coolness in the shadows as they fall upon the wall
And we're glad the turf is ready as the leaves begin to fall.

There's a longer sleep o'morning with no call to break our dreams
And a touch of frost is noticed at the edges of the streams
There's a blue mist on the bogland where the lonely curlews call
Saying winter time is coming when the leaves begin to fall.

The cows come home to milking as if glad to have a roof
And the horses take it easy putting down a slower hoof
There is bedding in the stables and there's fodder in the stall
And there's peace around the farm when the leaves begin to fall.

The springtime brings us beauty but it brings hard labour too
What with ploughing and with seeding and a hundred jobs to do
And in summertime a body has no chance for rest at all
Until August days are over and the leaves begin to fall.

O then a home is pleasant with a door to bar the wind
The plough and harrow idle and the harvest off our mind
With potatoes picked and pitted from the big ones to the small
Sure a man may well be happy when the leaves begin to fall.

13

Bonfire night in Ireland

'Tis Bonfire night in Ireland, God but the years go fast,
And here's myself a lonesome man who lives but in the past,
The long day's work is over and stars come out above
But sure they're not the stars of home, the ones I used to love;
And neither is this burning night like that old night in June
When Tommy Casey whistled up "The Rising of the Moon".

Sure that same boy could make the dead get up and stir their feet,
I'd rather spend an hour with him than all I drink or eat,
Beginning soft and easy with "The Harp" or "Shrule Aroon"
'Tis soon he'd have you fighting mad with some old Fenian tune;
But when he'd start the "Rocky Road" or "Humours of Glandore"
A blind and bothered cripple couldn't help but welt the floor.

Oh, Lord, those nights in Ireland with the meadows ripe to mow
And corncrakes' voices telling you old things of long ago.
I can see the big moon rising now, a globe of silver white,
I can smell the hawthorn blossoms here across this scorching night,
Aye, flinging all the years behind, I live that night in June
When Tommy Casey whistled up "The Rising of the Moon".

With our kippeens on our shoulders where our fathers' pike were drawn
We marched about the ashes as the day began to dawn,
And the call of all the ages flung its challenge in our face
As we pledged our lives to Ireland and the glory of the race;
And there stood Tommy Casey whistling up to Heaven the tune,
That made us freemen for a while, "The Rising of the Moon".

Oh, well, 'tis all a memory now and I'm a lonesome man,
While Tommy Casey sleeps tonight below by San Juan,
Aye, sure he died for liberty for when she lifts her hand
What better henchmen has she than the sons of that old land,
Whose lives and souls and deeds for her have woven such wondrous tune
That Gabriel's trumpet knows by now "The Rising of the Moon!"

'Tis Bonfire Night in Ireland, and the hawthorn still is sweet,
While Murphy's crossroads echo to the thrill of dancing feet;
There's laughter, love, and music, and a big moon shining white,
But, O, my God, the weary miles that part us all tonight.
And there is none to take his place, who stood that night in June,
And made us freeman for a while with "The Rising of the Moon."

Cappagh Hill

'Twas just last night a dream I had
'tis strange how dreams can thrill
I dreamt I was a little lad
Beyond on Cappagh Hill.
'Twas neither cap nor coat I had
For summer days were fair,
And I was just a happy lad
Among the meadows there.

I saw the village roofs below,
The beeches green and cool,
The paths through Cullen's fields that go
Along the way to school.
I heard my mother's voice ring clear,
And then-I woke to know
The crash of Broadway on my ear
For that was long ago.

Cappagh Hill

The boy from County Down

A boy with the dreams of a man was he, a lad from a lonesome place,
And he turned away from his family the width of the world to face;
Light of pocket and heavy of heart he started from Newry town
And his soul grew sick as he paused to part from the meadows of County Down.

He set his bundle beside the road and looked with a sob of pain
To the Mourne mountains and all abroad where he never might come again;
Then plucking a primrose from the hedge for spring was green on the sod,
He fared away on his wanderings with his fate in the hands of God.

O, many a tear did his mother weep in Rosaries said for him
And his father's sorrow looked wide and deep from eyes that were growing dim,
But the boy who parted from County Down was out in the world of men
Seeking the wealth in a far off town that should carry him home again.

Then when the hair on his head was white and the step of him faint and slow
Said he 'tis back by the morning's light to the land of my youth I'll go,
Though my parents both in the graveyard be and the noon of my life is set
sure County Down is the same, said he, and the mountains are standing yet.

He journeyed back from the world of men and the soul in him leaped with joy
To see the Mourne mountains again and the fields where he roamed a boy.
But sure he had toiled to the doors of doom in many a far off town
And he died when the primrose buds were in bloom by the hedges of County
Down.

The Cuckoo's call

O, what is it I'm dreaming of from weary day to day?
'Tis spring beyond in Ireland and me so far away.
And what is it I'm hearing clear above the city's glare -
Och sure it is the cuckoo's call at home in old Kildare.

Spring is there in Ireland with lambs upon the hills
And rainy breezes playing with the yellow daffodils,
Primroses peeping by the hedge and daisies everywhere
While thrushes sing their songs of love from greening bushes there.

Across the wild Atlantic it is beating on my lips
That little wind of April like a baby's fingertips,
'Tis driving me to madness for the things I want today
With spring beyond in Ireland and me so far away.

'Tis beating on my heartstrings and beating on my breast
Calling me to Ireland with a cry that will not rest,
To budding branch and bramble and sloe trees glimmering white
And little streams that whisper there down every wind of night.

O, greening heart of Ireland three thousand miles from me
My arms to you are reaching out across the salty sea;
The cuckoo's call rings through my blood across the world 'tis blown
For spring is there in old Kildare and I'm alone, -alone.

Hallow Eve colcannon

There's many a thing I'm missing since I sailed from County Cork,
    And many a thing I'm wanting midst the plenty of New York;
    I miss old friends and customs, and miss with many an ache
    The Hallow Eve colcannon that my mother used to make.

    I'm boarding in a restaurant, a stylish one at that,
    A frenchman takes my order while a darky takes my hat;
    And, faith, the dime or nickel that gets by that nimble pair
    Is fit to win a sweepstake on the Curragh of Kildare.

    I've wrestled with Kartufflin, I've tackled pomme de terre,
    Till I feel my Irish rising when I scan a bill of fare;
    I've left my malediction on Hungarian, Greek and Jew,
    Whose cooking shames the memory of the decent spud I knew.

    'Tis well I mind the mornings when I'd take my spade and go
    To the field beside the boreen where the big ones used to grow;
    How I'd whistle to the robins, or I'd mock the plover's cry,
    Getting many a rainy polthogue from the big clouds sailing by.

    You may talk of shining nuggets, sure they're fine to dig and see;
    But a laughing Irish "Murphy'" is a good as gold to me.
    For were you cold or hungry your gold were poor, I know,
    To the Hallow Eve colcannon that I had ten year ago.

Did you ever eat colcannon made with thickened cream,
And the greens and scallions blended like the pictures in a dream?
Did you ever scoop a hole on top to hold a melting cake
Of the clover flavoured butter that your mother used to make?

Did you ever eat and eat, afraid you'd let the ring go past
And some old married sprissaum pounced on it at the last?
Did you ever go blindfolded round the five plates in a row
And find a rosary beads three times, as I did long ago?

Myself and Pat MacCarthy were the lads that led the play.
He's down in South Australia now, a leading man they say;
But faith for fun and devilment that boyo had no peer,
When the pooka came to Bandon in the fading of the year.

Indeed, I'm not complaining for I've plenty and to spare,
And there's nowhere like America for one to win his share.
I go through life contented, but November brings an ache
For the Hallow Eve colcannon that my mother used to make.

O, Isle of mine

O, Isle of mine where the seas are sighing,
'Tis you are searing my soul with pain,
You who are holding me, living or dying,
With the grip of a loving that loves in vain.
For though the clouds in your skies are massing
Soft rains to fall on your breast like dew,
The stars above in their age long passing
Are marking the roads that I go from you.

O, Isle of mine where the sunset lingers
With soft sweet kisses on leaf and sod,
As though 'twas fearing to loose its fingers
From things so dear to the heart of God.
O, tender Isle, where the dawn comes breaking
The mists before her with slow footfall,
Sure the inmost core of my soul is aching
To sit beside you and know it all.

O, brave old Isle, with your face undaunted
Set skywards still where the winds are free,
Sure many a man by your loving haunted
Is walking alone through the lands like me.
Dreaming we are of trusty rifles
To voice our hate for your foes outhurled,
But the stranger's toil at our elbow stifles
The cries that we fling you across the world.

O, Isle of mine where the ancient glories
Of ages linger by hill and dell,
The harper's song and the Druid stories,
The old traditions that poets tell.
Never a stranger's hand could fashion
A love to better the love we knew,
Whose faith and fancy and hope and passion
Oh, grá mo chroí we have left with you.

O, Isle of mine where the winds are beating
A mystic tally of things to be,
The stars above in their nightly greeting
Are telling a wondrous tale to me.
"Behold," they cry and their acclamation
Is echoed again from the Throne Divine,
"You shall kiss the feet of her yet, a Nation"-
O, Soul of the soul of me, Isle of mine.

The land where the fairies play

When the cry of the restless city
Is stilled, at the close of day,
And lights are lit, I am dreaming of it-
The land where the fairies play.

And I see with a far off seeing
Unfettered by moon or sun,
A trail that goes where no mortal knows
When wearisome day is done.

Maybe it is Irish heather
Is singing the song I hear,
In a passion of April weather,
With June her lover, anear;
Maybe it is but the shiver
Of winds in a woodbine spray,
But it calls me far where the shamrocks are,
To the land where the fairies play.

O, there does the dawn come golden
Whatever the boon she'll bring
For, harvest or sowing that olden
Grey land is a land of Spring;
And the angels themselves in passing
Lean down with a kiss to say,
"She's the fairest sod that is known to God,
The land where the fairies play".

When spring with her dewy fingers
Strews flowers along the hills,
And a promise of a Maytime lingers
In the heart of the daffodils;
When soft winds wistfully follow
The pathways of winter grey,-
Does your soul soar back o'er the same old track
To the land where the fairies play?

If ever a drop of Erin
Is coursing along your veins,
You know of the smile she's wearing
This day through her April rains;
You know how the cuckoo's calling
Through woods where the young leaves sway,
When day sinks down o'er the mountains brown
Of the land where the fairies play.

For sure with its mystic haunting
It comes o'er the seas alway,
With a passionate sense of wanting
In the newer and larger day;
And it draws us ever and ever
As the call of a mother may,
To the green old land, to the grey old land,
The land where the fairies play.

Glenashee

The little lane of Glenshee runs down between the hills,
In spring 'tis like a road of gold with whins and daffodils;
'Tis just the width of Murphy's cart from grassy side to side
And there I came with Barney Flynn when first I was his bride.

My kin were mountain people all, and hard the life we had,
But Barney, over six feet tall, was just a farming lad.
We had a house and garden and a cow to give us milk,
And many an upland colleen said, "bedad you'll walk in silk."

'Twas little use for silk I had, on Barney's clean swept floor,
With Barney's children through the years to play beside our door.
And where was gold in all the world to match the gold we'd see
When spring brought whins and daffodils to us in Glenashee!

But what's the use of talking now, there'e gone beyond my call,
My fine strong man, my children three, my house and cow and all.
I'm just a wandering woman now and what you give to me
Is like the many a bite and sup I gave in Glenashee.

But somehow, when the spring comes by with laughter on her mouth
And winds that fair deludher you are blowing from the south,
'Tis yellow whins and daffodils along a lane I see,
A lane the width of Murphy's cart, at home in Glenashee.

Joggin' into Naas

Joggin' into Naas my lad, joggin' to the fair,
Sure many a pleasant day I had when I was younger there;
Along the road from Timahoe with darkness on my face
I'd start before the first cock crow,
Joggin' into Naas.

A load of good black turf I'd have, or else a pig or two,
A crate of fowl, a little calf and butter fresh as dew,
And then 'twould be "God save ye Tim" from neighbours everyplace
As day came breaking soft and dim
Along the road to Naas.

And sure 'tis often we'd be pressed by friendly farmers there
To stop a while and take a rest, myself and Moll the mare.
And many's the steaming cup of tea I've lifted to my face
From some good natured "Bean a Tí"
Along the road to Naas.

'Twas pleasant meeting neighbouring men and swapping country chat
For papers then were far between and hard to get at that.
And pleasant sure it was to go Stravagin' around the place
For fairings for herself at home,
When I'd get back from Naas.

Aye an old man loves to talk of things long past away,
But though 'tis feeble grows my walk, I had my time and day
Along the road from Timahoe, when dawning lit my face,
And joggin' to the fair I'd go,
Joggin' into Naas.

The Old Schoolhouse

The little bare feet

Over the fields I hear them pass
In the morning time, when the air is cool,
Along the paths through the tangled grass,
The little bare feet that trudge to school.

I hear them patter across the stile,
I hear them running a race to be
First at the picking of fruit awhile
In the shadows under the old crabtree.

I wake at dawn to the song of the lark,
'Tis then the meadows are dewy and sweet;
You see I'm a creature that's old and dark
And I long for the sound of the children's feet.

But glad or sorry, or swift or slow,
If the day be hot or the day be cool,
I watch for the time when they come and go,
The little bare feet that trudge to school.

The Old Bog Road

My feet are here on Broadway this blessed harvest morn
But O, the ache that's in them for the sod where I was born;
My weary hands are blistered from toil in cold and heat
And 'tis O, to swing a scythe today through fields of Irish wheat.
Had I a choice to journey back or own a king's abode
'Tis soon I'd see the hawthorn tree by the old bog road.

When I was young and innocent my mind was ill at ease
Through dreaming of America and gold beyond the seas,
Och, sorrow take their money but 'tis hard to get that same
And what's the whole world to a man when no one speaks his name
I've had my day and here I am with building bricks for load
A long three thousand miles away from the old bog road.

My mother died last springtime when Ireland's fields were green,
The neighbours said her waking was the finest ever seen,
There were snowdrops and primroses piled up around her bed
And Ferns Church was crowded when her funeral Mass was said.
And here was I on Broadway with building bricks for load
When they carried out her coffin from the old bog road.

There was a decent girl at home who used to walk with me,
Her eyes were soft and sorrowful like moonbeams on the sea,
Her name was Mary Dwyer,- but that is long ago
And the ways of God are wiser than the things a man may know.
She died the year I left her, but with building bricks for load
I'd best forget the times we met on the old bog road.

Och, life's a weary puzzle, past finding out by man,
I take the day for what it's worth and do the best I can,
Since no one cares a rush for me what need to make a moan,
I go my way and draw my pay and smoke my pipe alone.
Each human heart must know its grief though bitter be the load
So God be with old Ireland and the old bog road.

The old fireside

'Tis sitting by the stove I am where all the fire in sight
Would never raise a blister on a baby's arm tonight.
The wind goes tearing down the street as though the imps below
Were out upon a picnic playing ball with sleet and snow;
But I am seeing in my mind a hearthstone broad and wide
And a pile of Irish turf ablaze on the old fireside.

One side my mother sits and knits a stocking meant for me
My father's in the corner seat, his paper on his knee
A candle on the shelf beside gives all the light he needs
And granny's praying for I hear the rattle of he beads.
And there's myself with naked shins a happy boy beside
The blessed heat and comfort of the old fireside.

Sometimes the wind and rain comes down the chimney with a shout
And mother signs the Cross to see the ashes dance about,
And father laughs and says "bedad the pooka's out tonight,"
And granny whispers "hush avic, some poor soul's on its flight."
And then we get to thinking of the lonesome ones denied
For evermore the comfort of the old fireside.

The latch keeps lifting now and then as neighbours saunter in
With many a kind "God save all here" and "God save you again,"
And soon from talking politics at fairy tales they'll be;
With stools drawn up around the hearth as close as close can be
Then no one wants to look behind afraid a ghost might hide
Among the flickering shadows of the old fireside.

I wonder where they are tonight, for sure when all is told
'Tis feeling out of place they'd be on shining streets of gold;
But in the many mansions of the Father's house above
There may be humble corners where the poor can feel His love,
So in some friendly place apart where all their tears are dried
I know I'll meet my neighbours by God's own fireside.

The old home latch

At the bend of the road in Wicklow
With the glow of the hills around,
There's a bit of a whitewashed cabin there
Set snug in a plot of ground,
A lilac blooms by the doorway,
And swallows build in the thatch,
And 'tis many a time I'm longing
To be lifting the old home latch.

Sometime I shall leave the city,
Where the best in a man soon dies,
And seek for the tender pity
That broods in my native skies;
And be it in spring or summer,
Or be it in joy or pain,
I'll be glad with a mighty gladness
When I'm lifting that latch again.

For what is the city's luring,
The calling of street or mart,
When a wind from the hills of Wicklow
Is blowing across your heart?
And where can you find contentment
In a world of striving men
When a white-capped mother in Ireland
Is praying you home again.

Sure many a time and often
Where the Rockies loomed to the sky,
I've dreamed of her saying her Rosary
As the breezes of night went by;
And I knew that the Lord who heard her
Was setting my homeward track,
For the sake of a mother in Ireland
Who wanted her garsún back.

And so from the weary toiling
Of many an ill starred road
I will go where the hills of Wicklow
Are blowing their peace abroad;
For over the seas I'm seeing
A súgán chair by the fire,
At home in my fathers country,
The land of my heart's desire.

When the lilac tree is in blossom
And the hedges are green again,
I will go to my mother in Ireland
From a world of toiling men;
And I know that the tears will blind me
And the sob of my soul will catch
The breath from my lips, when I'm hearing
The click of that old home latch.

A little field

I know a little field girt by dripping hedges
Where, like truant children, snowflakes linger still;
Willywag and meadow lark through its wavy sedges
All day play their fill.

Rabbits patter here and there, timid, yet unfearing,
Kindly feet are those that through its paths pass to and fro,
Tenderest of tender winds that fan the breast of Erin,
The wind that it's four sides know.

If you'd put your ear down to its heart and listen
Wondrous things you'd hear within my far field stirring;
Snowdrops dressing up for birth, budding grass aglisten,
May moths' wings a whirring.

Tippytoe you'd hear them go whispering to each other
Daffodils, buttercups, cowslips and primroses,
Fearful lest when they should still be sleeping, earth their mother,
Find awake her posies.

Soon across my little field sunbeams will be falling,
From the rosy hands of spring silver rains will rattle,
Bulging shrill through pine and larch soon will March be calling
Lusty winds to battle.

I know a little field be it in God's keeping!
Over ocean roadways it's many a mile today,
There a twisted whitethorn heavy yet with sleeping,
Dreams, amid the lingering snow, of hawthorn spray.

The old boreen

Do you remember the old boreen that is many a mile away,
And the rushy pool where the shades lay cool at the close of a summer day?
Do you remember the robin's song in the hawthorn hedge that grew
By the garden gate that so long must wait for a homecoming sight of you?

Oh, do you remember the low white house with its coating of yellow thatch,
The earthen floor and the open door that swung to a ready latch,
The fire of turf and a cheery hearth where you gathered at evenings fall,
The dresser shelf with it's shining delph and the old clock on the wall?

Come, let us away from the noisy town, the clamour of crowded marts;
We will go to where the pulse of life beats low to the music of quiet hearts,
Where comcrakes shrill through the scented dust and dew-drenched meadows are sweet,
And the green green sod, like a balm from God hath healing for tired feet.

Down the winding ways of the old boreen we will wander on spirit wings,
While the haunted air like a mystic's prayer is aquiver with nameless things
The crickets will chirp a welcome home and the daisies look up to see,
While the long long years, they have drained our tears shall fall from us, you and me.

We will make our way to the fairies well, for deep in it's crystal flow
May linger gleams of those broken dreams we left in the long ago;
Gazing again in it's murmuring deeps we may see in a blinding light
The carefree ways of our childhood days shine out to our souls tonight.

Then when the low moon sinks in the west, and the thrill of the dawn is at hand,
We will wing our flight with the dying night to the shores of this other land;
But the strength and peace of our reveries and the balm of the sod so green
Will ease the strife of our exiled life so far from the old boreen.

The old road home

I would know it in the darkness were I deaf and dumb and blind,
I would know it o'er the thrashing of a million miles of foam,
I would know it sun or shadow, I would know it rain or wind,
The road that leads to Ireland, the old road home.

Sure the angels up in heaven would be pointing it to me
From every track that man has made since first he learned to roam,
And my feet would leap to greet it like a captive thing set free
The road that leads to Ireland the old road home.

I would find the hawthorn bushes, I would find the boreen's gap
With one old cabin standing 'mid the soft greening loam,
If the world was all a jumble in the great Creator's lap
I would know the road to Ireland, the old road home.

Farm, Yard

Owney the fiddler

I am Owney the fiddler,
Owney, blind and alone,
The loving of wife and children
I never can call my own;
But there isn't a road in Ireland
Or a boreen but I've trod,
Owney, the poor old fiddler,
Who soon will be gone to God.

I am Owney the fiddler,
And the little tunes that I play
By day or dark you'll be hearing
Though half of a world away;
For the four high Saints of Erin
And the four lords of the sea
And the four wise men of the fairy folk
Have whispered them to me.

I walk with never a stumble
Where many with sight go slow,
For I have a light within me
That only "the dark" can know.
The sun and moon and stars are my friends,
The rain on my face is sweet,
And where is there finer flooring
Than the grass under Owney's feet?

When I hear the birds in the bushes
I'm seeing them every one;
The wren like a fine soft April day,
The lark like a rising sun;
There's the blackbird mellow as moonrise,
The thrush like a wooing lover;
But the robin is sweet as rest to my feet
When a long, hard day is over.

I am Owney, the fiddler,
Who never had eyes to see,
But the great high spirits of Erin
Have whispered my tunes to me;
And whether it was in mornin'
Or duskin' you heard me play,
You'll think of Owney the fiddler
Over half of a world away.

Takin' tay at Reillys

Arrah, did you know the Reilly's that lived near Donadea?
A fine old fashioned place they had as snug as snug could be,
And sure for decent people you couldn't beat them round
The two and thirty counties of Ireland's blessed ground.

'Tis often I am thinking of Sundays after Mass
When down the mossy boreen that skirts their door I'd pass,
And "Come inside and rest yourself agra," herself would say,
And then we'd have potato cake and a cup of Irish tay.

Such tay it was, with cream, bedad, and plenty more in sight,
And sure the hot potato cake I'm tasting here tonight,
It was buttered in the middle with the butter running through
And faith with all respects to you my face was buttered too.

My stomach's sick and tired of the food 'tis getting now
With "butterine" and milk in tins that never saw a cow,
And once a woman said to me "I always take my tay
With a slice of lemon in it for that's the Russian way."

I never was a Russian, a Frenchman or a Jew,
I'm Irish every inch of me and my tastes are Irish too,
I like a dish of cabbage with corned beef or pork
But O, for hot potato cake I'd go from here to Cork.

And Bridget Reilly was the one to make you drink and eat,
You'd never leave her table while a crumb was on your plate,
She never kept an empty pot or griddle on her floor
Or shut against a neighbour's face the latchpin of her door.

It isn't gold I'm wanting, though money's good you know,
And sure my health is fine, thank God as twenty years ago.
But I'm lonesome for the Reillys, this many a weary day
And I'm hungry for potato cake and a cup of Irish tay.

To a sod of turf

In you the beauty that old springtimes knew –
Leaves that were green when Tara was in prime,
Blossoms once diamond with morning dew
Were wed in death upon the lap of time.

Here is the laughter of wind rippled grass,
The fragrance of a clover scented sod,
Caught in the web of years and born to pass
Into the endless processes of God.

I wonder if a Druid's sunrise prayer
Is echoing still amongst your fibres brown,
That maybe were oak leaves in Kildare
'Ere Rome was built or Liffey knew a town.

Within your whispering flame may yet perchance,
Linger the echoes of old music gone;
Bugles of Dé Danainn or throb of dance
On Bealtaine eve upon a starlit lawn.

But Daghda is gone young Aengus is asleep;
The wheeling centuries passed them long ago,
While stone and sod their ancient records keep
Till ends their cycle. It is written so.

When I was leaving Ireland

When I was leaving Ireland the leaves were falling down,
 A dreary mist was drifting above old Derry town;
 The sun itself was cloudy and frosty was the wind
 When I was leaving Ireland who left my soul behind.

When I was leaving Ireland my parents wept full sore,
 The kindly neighbours gathered to bless me o'er and o'er,
 I clung around the doorway, I gazed on sky and sod
 When I was leaving Ireland that bitter day of God.

When I was leaving Ireland I watched the shore line dip
 Beyond the darkening waters that surged about the ship,
 Then with a cry of longing none heard save heaven on high,
 My soul sped back to Ireland to linger till I die.

And there at home in Ireland it is this blessed day
 Though both my parents dead and gone have found their house of clay;
 It sees the dawns and twilights, it feels the winds and rain
 And when I go to Ireland I'll find that soul again.

It may be that in living some ship may bear me o'er,
 It may be that in dying the Saviour I adore
 Will bid a kindly angel convey me to the sky
 O'er some old road in Ireland I trod in years gone by.

But I'll go back to Ireland in life or death I'll go,
 For there my soul is waiting with all the loves I know;
 By windy dawns 'tis waiting and twilight's grey with rain
 And I must go to Ireland to find that soul again.

Tom Moore

How are you faring now, Tom Moore,
In the mystic land of the dead
Where never the Harp of Tara's Hall
May round you its music shed!
While a young May moon is shining high
Over Lough Neagh's banks tonight
Erin, with the tear and smile in her eye
Still holds your memory bright.

How is it with you now, Tom Moore,
Where your starry soul has flown
And where never a rose that summer knows
Is left to wither alone!
Oft in the stilly night we sing
Your songs like a lilted prayer
While lovers a dream by Bendemeer's stream
Hearken and hail them there.

The waters that meet in Avoca's glen
Still sing as sweet as of old
Though far from the land of his countrymen
Their Poet lies dead and cold.
O, believe me if all the endearing charms
Of the world were ours today
We'd gather them as a wreath in our arms
To lay on your sacred clay.

O, Moore tho' far from the land of your birth
You bade the world goodbye
And though sorrow your young days shaded, yet
There's a young moon in the sky.
And Nora Creina's eyes still smile
By Bann and Liffey and Suir.
As in the days when you sang the lays
Of Ireland's soul, Tom Moore.

What Ireland is

Sure Ireland's not a country
In this world to me at all,
It is just an emerald fringing
Of the Blessed Virgin's shawl.
'Tis a blend of furze and heather
And a primrose scented sod
Since the first stars sang together
Their morning song to God.

And I'd rather be in Ireland
This fine summer day
Than sitting on the throne of Spain
With premiers on my pay;
And I'd rather far be carrying
Potatoes on my back
Than, with politicians worrying,
Rule England's Woolsack.

O, the green sod of Ireland
Is kindly to the hand,
And a fool he'd be to leave it
To head a king's command;
For what has glory in it
When a man's heart is sore
For the lilting of a linnet
By his own cabin door!

Sure peace is not in riches
Or what they can bring
A man in tattered breeches,
May far outrank a king.
So with a roof above me
Of good Irish thatch
I will live in holy Ireland
Until death lifts the latch.

Kerry

O 'tis over beyond in Kerry the roots of my heart are set,
And 'tis over beyond in Kerry the dreams of my life are yet,
Sure the spirit was broken in me that desolate winter's morn
When I turned away from Kerry, where I and my race was born.

The sun was hid in the heavens, the wind with a wild unrest
Was moaning among the shadows, a rain cloud swung in the west;
There was no glimmer of brightness, no shining on earth or sky
When I kissed the sod of Kerry, in a long and a last goodbye

Ochón!, ochón, for Kerry, if wishes were sails and ships
'Tis I would be speeding to you with songs of joy on my lips.
Sore sick of the exile's roving I'd go where my youth was passed
To ease the ache in my bosom and sleep with my own at last.

My hands are so weary of toiling always on the stranger's floor,
There are no smiles on the faces I see by the stranger's door.
'Tis little for me they're caring and little of them I know
And the core of my heart is lonesome for Kerry and long ago.

For the old thatched home of my father, the turf fires warm and bright,
The pleasant song and the story when neighbours dropped in at night,
The wild bogs purple with heather, the ring of the crossroads set
For dancing on summer evenings to tunes that I can't forget.

Sure all day long am looking at pictures like these instead
Of the busy wonderful city where I earn my scanty bread,
Thinking 'tis whitewashed cabins I'm seeing on Broadway Street,
And the old road down to Killarney under my aching feet.

Oh, nowhere in all the world is the grip of a hand so true,
Or the lilt of a laugh so cheering as Kerry, a stór, with you.
Misty with rain and sunshine, and filled with songs of the sea,
Like fairy music at midnight, you're calling the heart from me.

Calling and haunting and calling, like the ghost of my mother gone,
While every vein of my Irish heart leans out to you dark and dawn.
O, home of the silver waters, kingly and kind and true
God Bless you old County Kerry, for He never made match for you.

Kildare

Say, what of Kildare –is she waking or sleeping
Now the day of our testing is growing apace?
And mighty as winter tossed billows onleaping
Wild "farrahs" ring out from the lips of our race!
What of Kildare, ever foremost and ready,
Whenever our warflag was raised for the right,
Has she lifted her standard, true hearted and steady,
Where Kildare ought to be - in the thick of the fight?

The shrine of St Brigid whose Lamp ever burning
Shone out like the star on the ramparts of God,
The home of Lord Edward, our eagle of morning -
Could traitors abide on so sacred a sod!
Could fear of defeat or despair of a morrow
Find place where the ashes of Tone at are rest
Is there room for a coward or time for a sorrow
With 'Croom a boo' watchword and oak tree for crest!

From Naas to Maynooth rings the slogan of "Freedom."
From Newbridge to Leixlip, Kilcock to Athy,
The men of Cilldara are there when we need them
They know how to fight and they know how to die.

There the spirit of liberty hovers unsleeping
Where rebels and martyrs found birth and a grave,
And the murdered of Mullaghmast watch still are keeping
O'er fields never trod by the foot of a slave.

Sure the challenge she threw in the face of the foemen
Of old when her clans flashed their falchions in air
Is still to the fore for a finish, and no man
Shall humble the shield of Fitzgerald's Kildare.
Unconquered, invincible, steadfast forever,
With a hand for the south and the north and the west
The foremost in onset, the latest to waver.
She stands with the counties, the first and the best.

Kildare is awake for she never has slumbered
Whenever the summons to battle went forth,
The deeds of her dead with the bravest are numbered
The sons of her soil are the salt of the earth.
As true as the Liffey that sweeps ever onward
Through sunshine and storming, through shadow and light.
Kildare holds her standard aloft in the vanguard
Where Kildare ought to be —in the thick of the fight.

Limerick

O, Limerick, Limerick, Limerick, your name on the tip of my tongue
Is sweeter than singing of linnets when May on the meadows is young,
'Tis kinder than dripping of honey or foaming of milk to the lips,
O, Limerick, Limerick, Limerick, my blessed old town of the ships.

As you sit on the banks of the Shannon, a Queen on a beautiful throne
You are sealing the right hand of Erin with the gem of the Treaty Stone,
And the kindness and loving good nature that fall from the shine of your face
Though spread o'er the rest of creation would leave us enough for the race.

Though over the ways of the world my feet may go lonesome and wild
'Tis ever the breast of the mother is sweetest repose for the child;
So some day, please God I'll come jogging back to you with songs on my lips
O, Limerick, Limerick,Limerick, my blessed old town of the ships.

Old County Clare

O, Beannacht Dé leat go brách old County Clare to you.
From the roads that go by Ennis to the streets of Killaloe.
'Tis many a day I wandered there and drove my donkey's cart
By rows of hawthorn hedges that are scenting all my heart.

God made your face so beautiful and fashioned you so sweet,
No wonder I am longing for your sod beneath my feet.
No wonder I am wearying where dust and dryness be
For a windy April morning on the headlands of Kilkee.

O, Beannacht Dé leat go brách to all the ways I knew
From the roads around by Ennis to the streets of Killaloe;
'Tis I'll be going back some day to see the hawthorns there
And rest my weary bones with you, in good old County Clare.

Munster

A pleasant land is Munster now that spring is stepping by
With blossoms on the blackthorn and sunshine in the sky
O, beautiful is Munster where light and shadow play
Like little children out of school this blessed April day.

There's many a town in Munster I'm thinking of this minute
I'd empty out my pocket for the joy of walking in it
From Tipperary down to Cork, from Waterford to Clare
And never mind my stint of work if I were only there.

Belfast's a thriving city, but it moidhers me with noise
And there's no easy-going way about its girls and boys
They're fine and good and decent with a kind word on their tongue
But sure they're not the people that I knew when I was young.

There's grandeur in those Northern hills but proud and dark they seem
To one who's seeing Mangerton forever in a dream
And not a valley in the north in spite of all its charms
Could hold a homesick Munster man like his old Moher's arms.

Och, wisha for a seanchaí beside a Munster fire
With Tomaseen O'Sullivan to ease my heart's desire
When rain is tapping on the roof like jigs by Padna Flynn
And kindly hands to lift the latch and bid me welcome in.

There's many a mossy bank I know beside the River Lee
All yellow with primroses that is beckoning to me
'Tis there I'd take my fill of ease stretched on a grassy shawl
With not a factory whistle to be rousin' me at all.

Och, wisha for the Munster land I've left this many a year
And wisha for the Munster folk I'm holdin' still so dear
Some day I'll foot it back, please God, from Belfast toil and fret
To find again the Munster sod my heart cannot forget.

A song of Leitrim

Sing a song of Leitrim lad, of Leitrim in the morn
Where little lazy bits of wind are stirring up the corn;
When "arrah, but 'tis early yet" the sleepy grasses cry,
For Venus's gold petticoat is still upon the sky.
Sing a song of Leitrim lad, I keep it in my prayer
And the kindest face in Ireland inside a cabin there.

Sing a song of Leitrim with the big clouds trailing down
As fierce and wild as Fionn McCool until they reach the town;
And then 'tis with a laugh they go in rings of pearly mist
While sore you'd be to see them flee and leave you there unkissed.
Sing a song of Leitrim with the heather left and right
And the kindest face in Ireland that's gone to God tonight.

Sing a song of Leitrim where the day goes down to rest
Like the little baby foostering to find it's mother's breast.
Where the robin, like a garsún that is hard to get to bed,
Sings out "good night" a hundred times before he hides his head.
Sing a song of Leitrim with the mountains in a row,
And the kindest face in Ireland that I left there long ago.

Sing a song of Leitrim, of the old place, root and stem,
With the neighbours all about me and I just one of them;
Of the fine flaithiúlach women and the friendly farming men,
And the love I'll never know avic outside of it again.
Sing a song of Leitrim lad, the place I'll see no more
And my mother's face God rest her, beside the cabin door.

When it rains In Donegal

When it rains in Donegal, and sure 'tis often raining!
It isn't common rain at all but bits of diamond dew,
And it drips from Erin's eyelids like the blossoming and waning
Of the many years she's waiting for her dreaming to come true.
There's the yellow of a whin bush and the swish of heather in it,
The tang of lifting peat smoke and the plover's lonesome call;
When it rains in Donegal.

The laughing daisies love it as they dance along the causans,
White ducks with wings extended preen themselves in every pool,
The barefoot children seek it from the weeshiest of garsún's
To seekers after knowledge who trot their way to school.
Sure the robin sings his clearest and the mountains look their nearest.
And heaven itself seems bending down to give you friendly call,
A clean wind you'll be knowing and a clear road you'll be going
When it rains in Donegal.

O, When it rains in Donegal, and mostly it is raining!
Don't think 'tis getting wet you are or fret what you wear
While every drop is telling you new life and strength you're gaining
From the holy sod beneath you, and the things you're seeing there.
When it rains in Donegal, thank God for rainy weather!
'Tis happy you will find yourself though polthogues on you fall;
From Errigal to Muckish you'll step lightly as a feather
When it rains in Donegal.

Because He came

Because He came to us, a little Child,
Rebellious man with God was reconciled;
And burdened hearts felt rest was nigh to them
That night when angels sang o'er Bethlehem.

Because He came to save a fallen race
The Star of Hope shone white above our face,
And all the centuries that sped before
Were lit from Heaven's newly opened door.

A Christmas Blessing

May the right hand of God ever hold you in keeping
Through coming and going, through waking and sleeping,
May the love of the Christ Child your spirit be lighting
And the smile of His Mother your heart be delighting;
May Blessed St. Joseph be near you in sorrow,
And the high Saints of Erin be guarding your morrow,
May peace be your treasure, and long be your living,
With joy in good measure for taking and giving.
In friendship, go leor beyond bound or expressing
To your door I am sending this Christmas blessing.

The Holy Night

Upon the hills of Bethlehem
The wintry snow lay deep
With watchful men to shepherd them
Were folded flocks asleep
When one Wee Lamb of heavenly birth
The flower of Jesse's rod
Came down to save a sinful earth
And bring it back to God.

Now praises to the Baby hands
So soft on Mary's breast
That brought deliverance to the lands
So long by sin oppressed
Long were the years that lay before
And dark the years behind
But He unlocked His Father's door
That night for all mankind.

A thrill swept through the heart of night
The skies were all aflame
When out of uncreated Light
The Lord of glory came
And angels, winging overhead
Proclaimed redemption's morn
When, sheltered in a humble shed
The Son of God was born.

Hunting the wren

O, Don't you remember over in Ireland when you went hunting the wren,
And don't you wish you were over in Ireland this day of St. Stephen again?
But sure the white-lipped ocean is flowing in billows of drenching foam,
Between the way that your feet are going and the warm hearth lights of home.

'Twas Christmas time and the holly and ivy hung from rafter and wall,
And you slipped out to the garden slyly to answer your comrades' call,
Your mother looked up with a smile God bless her, your father stood by the door,
The firelight flickered on shelf and dresser and played on the earthen floor.

Outside the ways were rigid in winter, the skies were heavy with snow,
But you and the weather were friends together back there in the long ago.
Through hill and hollow and brake and brier you scrambled the whole day through,
Till the wee brown bird of your heart's desire was lost in the dark on you.

There were Matt and Pat and Maurice and Andy, there was Tim the leader of all,
There was Mike Malone who could flip a stone straight over a ten foot wall;
Brave lads o'er many a wearier way their feet have travelled since then,
But their hearts are as true to the past as you, when the wren days come again.

'Tis Christmas time in the Old Land now, there is brooding snow in the wind,
The turf light flickers on shelf and dresser with holly and ivy twined.
But you and I by the stranger's hearth think back to old times again,
To the dear home ways and the Stephen's days when we went hunting the wren.

A Little Boy

A Little Boy on sandalled feet
Came homeward from the village street;
His Mother having called Him said
"Play weary One 'tis time for bed"

Gravely He stood beside her chair
To chant His evening psalm and prayer,
Then putting by his toys, He went
To sleep till morning, well content.

Around Him there on wings of flame
Adoring hosts of angels came,
While warrior Michael with his sword
Kept watch beside the Living Word.

Above, through endless fields of space
The planets kept their tireless pace,
While He, their Lord, slept peacefully,
A little Child in Gallilee.

A New Year's resolve

The new year has come and the old year is over-
The snow o'er the earth spreads beautiful cover,
As spotless and pure as an angel's robe fair-
And nothing seems ugly, or grimy or bare.

The new year has come. 'Tis a time for beginning,
A time for new efforts, new victories winning:
The old page is finished, the new page is clear.
Let's make a good record this happy new year!

Life

Dead leaves lying heap on heap underneath the rain and wind,
Are you dreaming in your sleep of the summer left behind?
Are you restless for the spring now gone by where springs must go,
Lilt of song and whirr of wing that in May you used to know?

Gone the swallows from our hills, silent is the blackbird's call,
Gone the flash of daffodils, coldly now the shadows fall,
Soon will chilly fingered days write upon the withered grass,
Frosty records of the ways years must in their dying pass.

Dying! Is it death or birth; who shall say who only see
Something cherished flit from earth, knowing not what things may be;
These dead leaves beneath our feet trampled under wind and rain
May, by some unguessed of fate, leap to sentient life again.

He who gave the pulse of life to the lowliest things that are
Moulding them through stress and strife to bud and blossom, stone and star,
Will not cast to nothingness what His love in patience wrought,
They can surely ne'er be less that fruit of His eternal thought.

Round the wheels go ceaselessly, flesh to dust and leaf to mould,
But in God's great alchemy new life springing from the old,
Through the mighty mills of change all must pass as grist to be
Fitted for a loftier range waiting in eternity.

In the circle of the spheres naught is wasted, naught is lost,
Where until the light appears spirit matter-fraught is tossed;
All must seek and find their goal, change by change and breath by breath,
Clod and leaf and star and soul, for all is life, there is no death.

Rosary time

At the fall of the night in Ireland when spring in the land is fair,
At the fall of the night in Ireland when passionate June is there,
When woods are ruddy in autumn or hoary with winter's rime,
At the fall of the night in Ireland 'tis rosary time.

With book and beads in her fingers the mother goes to her place
The holy candle beside her, the peace of God in her face,
And out of their chosen corners the voices of children chime
At the fall of the night in Ireland, at rosary time.

Outside the song of the robin is hushed in his sheltered nest,
The wind with a rainy sweetness is sighing itself to rest,
The world with her old time longing swings low to a minor rhyme
At the fall of the night in Ireland, at rosary time.

Oh, many a dream of beauty shines up from the lowest sod
And many a golden duty binds men to the feet of God,
But the sorest passion of living is stilled to a chord sublime
At the fall of the night in Ireland, at rosary time.

To Saint Joseph

Where broods the Sphinx o'er Egypt's wild,
You spread with tender hands
A bed for Mary and her child
Upon the desert sands.
God's eyes down all His ages were
Upon them as they slept,
While you, their humble servitor,
A ceaseless vigil kept.

O Joseph of the mighty faith,
Whose axe and hammer true
Built many a home in Nazareth
That Jesus loved and knew,
Tell us what mighty answer broke
The Sphinx's centuried quest,
When Mary slumbered on your cloak
With Christ upon her breast.

A Saint Patrick's Day
memory

It is well as I grow older to have things to keep me warm,
A fire against the cold and a roof against the storm,
A memory, though it's dimming now, of other years gone by,
And a well of laughing water lit by a blue March sky.

There were tall ash trees about it where the building thrushes sang
And the merry winds of springtime all their bells of music rang
And the little path beside it that I trod for pails of water
Was spangled with green shamrocks gay as an Ard Rí's daughter

Oh, the ripple of that water as it bubbled from the earth
Sure it sounded like the singing of young stars swung out from birth
And I mind the willywagtails sipping at the crystal flood
As if an angel beckoned and God said that it was good.

And 'twas there I gathered shamrocks over such a waste of years
That I cannot see them clearly for the haze of lonely tears
But I'm missing not the shamrocks for they still are blooming there
But the light of youth behind me and the times I knew no care.

St. Patrick's Day

Now is the time when our homing swallows
Put out to sea for their native hills
There's a flash of green in the woodland hollows,
The ways are starry with daffodils.
There's a veil of white on the blackthorn bushes,
A flame of gold on the bogland whin
The merry larks and the fluting thrushes
Their vernal chanting of love begins.

Young spring is coming in emerald sheathing
Her bugles ring down the echoing way
And winds grown sweet with her honeyed breathing
Blow in the dawn of Saint Patrick's Day.
Swing on o' earth through your dizzy spaces
Though sore your burden of strife and care
Sure peace is over the ancient places
Our Patrick shelters beneath his prayer.

His radiant spirit in Ulster lingers
And Leinster, Munster and Connaught sod
He blesses today with loving fingers
Dipped in the boundless founts of God;
He wakes unseen where the young grass shivers
Across the Isle that he made his own
By the healing wells and the storied rivers,
The fruitful field and the warm hearthstone.

On the quiet dead in the churchyard sleeping
He sets the seal of his saving sign
And whispers "Oh harvest of my reaping
In earth and heaven you still are mine"
And so when the swallows are homeward faring
A new life quickens in leaf and clod
Saint Patrick pledges anew to Erin
His love in the name of the true God.

Carraig an Aifrinn

By the side of a road in Kerry
Where winds from the ocean cry
There's a rock in a sheltered hollow
Thrice holy from years gone by;
A sentinel angel guards it,
And will until Gabriel's call
Summons the dead and living
On that day that is last of all.

For there in a godless era
Came the hunted priest to his own
To offer the Lamb of sacrifice
Here on this altar stone;
When men like wild beasts tracked him
With rack and fire and sword
He fed to his tortured people
The bread of the Living Lord.

With cold and hunger upon them,
And terrors to hem them round,
They kept their tryst with their Saviour
Here on this sacred ground;
But the hosts of God were with them,
And Patrick's prayer was beside,
And Mary who stood on Calvary
When her Son was crucified.

If

If I were home in Ireland, but sure 'tis far away,
I'd ramble up to Derry to pass a pleasant day.
And then light footed as a lark that bathes in morning dew
I'd make a call in Donegal and the Glens of Antrim too.

If I were home in Ireland God make my dreaming true,
I'd travel down to Galway and holy Arran too.
I'd hold in Connemara, high speech with them who know
What magic to my land was given, by the High Ones long ago.

If I were home in Ireland beside the lovely Lee,
Where Shandon bells are pealing still their notes so wild and free.
I'd pray for great MacSwiney's soul who stripped of earthly dross
Stood in God's judgement hall as bare as Christ upon the cross.

If I were home in Ireland, to Leinster I would go,
Where grows the grass of Tara above a court laid low.
Where great King Cormac ruled of old I'd touch with reverent lips
And then I'd go to Dublin and Liffey of the Ships.

Through the town of Dublin I'd wander up and down,
Among the many places I hold in high renown.
From Murphy's house in Thomas Street, where young Lord Edward died,
I'd go where Pearse and Connolly and Clarke lie side by side.

If I were home in Ireland, for 'tis my homeland still,
Although I never saw it and maybe never will.
I'd spill the loving of my soul as roses spill their scent,
On the olden land of my desire, and so be well content.

The croppies grave

Under the Lia Fail they lie, quiet and lone and still,
Where the winds of the world are roaming o'er the summit of Tara hill;
Quiet and still and lonely with the things that have ceased to be,
Under the Lia Fail they lie, the Stone of our destiny.

Under the Lia Fail, O God, where the throne of our kings was set,
And even the mould remembers the days of their glory yet;
Under the Lia Fail that lifts its shoulder above the sod
Like some high beacon of majesty that summons the eye to God.

O, lonely it is in Tara where the beating of rain is known,
And only the kine are sentinels by the place of our Crowning Stone;
Where down in the dreary darkness of things that have ceased to be
Our murdered croppies are lying 'neath the Stone of our destiny.

King and soldier and lordly knight, turret and door and hall,
Bard and lover and lady bright, what lives of your life at all?
A marking ridge in the sheathing grass, a mound by the Lia Fail
And a wind going by like a Banshee's cry o'er the broken dreams of the Gael.

Aye, but that wind of Tara has swept over Aileach's Hall,
And the four high roads of the world that have known the deeds of us all;
It has kissed Ramillies and Fontenoy, it has swung through a dawning's flame
O'er a grave in the heart of Dublin that waits for a hero's name.

Behold, 'tis a mighty signal, that Stone of our destiny,
Sealing the Erin of ancient days to an Erin that is to be,
And where could a faithful croppy find holier resting place
Than here where the winds of Tara are blowing above his face?

Under the Lia Fail they lie, quiet and lone and still,
'Neath the crowning place of an Ard Rí on the summit of Tara hill;
And sure 'twas a fitting burial, for king of his race is he
Who flings his life on the altar stone of his country's liberty.

Casement

They took the title from his name,
That paltry gift of Britain's hand,
Nor saw a laurel wreath aflame
For him today in every land;
They stood him on a gallows tree
With eyes blindfolded from the light,
Nor saw, down all the years to be,
His soul a sword for truth and right.

They hanged him high in Pentonville;
Uncoffined there his ashes lie,
A mound of dust that may not thrill
To sun or shade, to sea or sky.
But somewhere, far beyond our ken,
O'er awful vistas yet unrolled,
That dust shall spring to fighting men
As sprang the dragons' teeth of old.

A Galahad of stainless name,
A knight unstained midst wrong and strife,
Their lies could not besmirch his fame,
Their rope could never end his life,
Their gallows was a pedestal
Lifting him up for all to see
How Irishmen yet fight and fall
And die for Ireland's liberty.

Fall as a wind tossed billow falls
To give new tides behind it place,
When the uprisen ocean calls
Its waters in a stormy race;
Fall as the martyrs of the world
Shall fall forever, fearlessly,
Till the last wrong to hell is hurled
And man, in God's high name, is free.

They murdered him in Pentonville
While howling mobs profaned the air
Like wolves who only dare to kill
When the full pack is gathered there;
But others, of his countrymen,
Knelt in the dust for him who cried;
"I give my life for Ireland," then
"God take my soul"- before he died.

God took his soul, God heard his cry,
God guaged his reckoning, yea, and set
Above the farthest reach of sky.
Casement's immortal coronet
God ranged his coin of sacrifice
His life, 'twas all he had to give
With theirs whose blood has paid our price,
And died that Ireland's soul shall live.

Ireland speaks

I am no beggar at your gate,
No suppliant for your mercy, I
Time looms insistent with my fate,
I live or freedom's self must die.

My name is red upon the screeds
By nations writ, from sire to son
My blood demands its title deeds
To every height by valour won.

You call me weak and old! Not so!
Eternal youth my soul sustains,
Nor tyrants' blight can chill the glow
Of ageless life that fires my veins.

Weak! I, whose naked hands have met
And matched your armies, blow for blow,
For nigh a thousand years, and yet
Stand here a conqueror! Nay, not so.

Down immemorial years I've trod
I looked on time when time was young
I taught to you the word of God
When language halted on your tongue.

My hand is on the helm of years,
My spirit holds the world in fee,
And still, above my night of tears
Flames God's North Star of liberty.

O blind ye are and dead to all
The ancient wisdom that I know-
Is it not writ that wrong must fall
Wherever faith and honour go?

Though crushed by centuries of scorn,
Be freedom's hand and freedom's word
Yet some red Resurrection morn
That hand will strike, that voice be heard.

"The Celt is gone and Ireland dead!"
So mocked ye in my hour of need.
Victors today my children tread
Upon the dust of Cromwell's seed.

Beyond the farthest ocean's sweep
Where once my kith and kin ye hurled
They and their children's children keep
My living rampart round the world.

I stand before your loaded guns,
Your bayonets press against my breast
Strike if you dare! My soldier sons
And God's strong hand will do the rest.

My banner flaunts down every wind,
It holds no serf, it knows no crown
'Tis freedom's call to all mankind,
And who shall dare to drag it down!

The lad who came home

They used to whisper of him
In the place where he was born,
The grasses and the wee wild things
That gossip in the morn;
One said, he used to love us well
But now he never comes
Since he put a flag above him
To the beating of the drums.

Then on a rainy evening
He was borne to them again,
To lie in death's great silence
In the shadow of the glen.
Wrapt in his country's flag was he,
Her drums his dirge did call.
The lad who had died for liberty
In the name of Donegal.

Parnell

Lift him up in the place of his people, let him stand where the crowds go by,
The man who was pledged for our liberty, the man who can never die,
O'er the streets of that ancient city where the breath of his soul was blown
Let him stand like a mighty Ard Rí that hovers above his own.

Let the lips that unleashed our passions and the hands that for us threw down,
The challenge of man for his liberty he set over Dublin town;
Let the dawn of our day be golden and the rain of our night be sweet
Where the glory and pride of Erin are wreathed about his feet.

Lift him up in the place of his people, let the surge of their love be hurled
To the face that was turned in strength to them from all the claims of the world,
While the nations of men are travailing in joy of a ransomed birth
Set him here where the Celt is fashioning the crown of his fate on earth.

Patriot, hero or demagogue, what matter the cry he met,
On the scroll of eternal liberty the place of his fame is set,
And there will the royal greatness that shadowed the might of kings
Be one with spirit of man that lies at the core of created things.

Lift him up in the place of his people, for the earth's soul quickens apace,
And the nations of men are standing heart riven and face to face
Gauging the dreams that a race may dare whatever that race may be,
For the tribes of God know but one free sod on the summits of liberty.

Lift him up in the place of his people, on the road that is free to men,
Where never a tyrant dares to flaunt the shame of our bands again;
O'er the streets of that ancient city where the breath of his soul was blown,
Let him stand like a mighty Ard Rí that hovers above his own.

A belated wooing

When he was twenty, Seán O'Flynn had his eyes upon the girls,
And he felt his young heart thumping at the sight of flowing curls,
But his father said, "be careful" and his mother said, "beware!"
So Seán dodged all the girls he met at market and at fair
.'Twas like a hermit there he was from everyone apart,
While little Bridie Heffernan was dancing through his heart.

When Seán O'Flynn was thirty he was a hermit still,
Although the money that he had a miser's sack would fill;
At fair and dance and gathering he always walked alone,
With not a smile upon his face no more than on a stone;
For little Bridie Heffernan, to please her parents, too,
Had married a big farming man outside of Killaloe.

When Seán O'Flynn was forty he married widow Dunn,
Who, fat and fair and farsighted, had picked a moneyed one.
She drove him night and morning, in sunshine and in rain,
Till Seán O'Flynn was sick and sore of matrimony's chain;
While little Bridie Heffernan, no better off than he,
With the farming man from Killaloe knew only misery.

When Seán O'Flynn was fifty he was alone again,
For the widow Dunn had passed beyond the world of living men.
And the farming lad from Killaloe had also slipped his rope,
So two belated lovers stood upon the hills of hope;
And when the heart of Seán met Bridie's Heffernan's heart
No locksmith ever known on earth could break their bonds apart.

A nature story

"Let us have peace," the tiger said,
as he gobbled up a giraffe;
"Let us have peace," the lion sighed,
as he gnawed the bones of a calf;
"Let us have peace," cried the jungle folk,
as they hunted in packs together –
But an elephant herd, to anger stirred,
Scattered them yon and thither.

A mouse, hot-footing from nearing slaughter,
Turned the elephants' blood to water,
But fierce eyed bird, with a venomous beak,
Grabbed the mouse without time for a squeak;
While a monkey, high in a bamboo tree,
Cried "the jungle's now safe for democracy".

Then a coconut fell on the monkey's head,
And the monkey arose, with eyes blood red,
And yelled "Let the lad who shook this tree
Come out for a tussle here with me,
And I'll swat him so hard in the solar plexus,
He'll find himself twenty miles south of Texas".

So, sad to relate, the story goes,
When peace is a thing to be won by blows,
And jungles war upon jungles until
There isn't anything left to kill;
And the last lone victor cries "Look at me!
I'm safe, I'm at peace, I'm democracy".

Jerry Connor's forge

By the crossroads of Knockallen where the bog and upland meet,
There's a tidy row of houses that the neighbours call "the street"
It is free and independent, though it pays its tax to George,
For it runs its own Home Parliament in Jerry Connor's forge.

In the quiet dusk of evening, when the iron hammer rings,
That mighty song of labour that has raised and routed kings,
The members take their places, with their backs against the wall,
And who but Jerry Connor should be leader of them all.

For the tangles of Westminster there's little patience there,
Where State affairs are settled in the shoeing of a mare;
And bills that Whig and Tory view with sinking of the heart
Are fixed while Jerry rims the wheel of Kelly's donkey cart.

'Tis there the Kaiser's law is scorned, the Czar is roundly cursed,
And every ruling head declared no better than the worst,
When the world around, from China to the Rockies farthest gorge,
Is tried before the Parliament in Jerry Connor's forge.

Pat Murphy is Conservative, and likes to hold his views,
Apart from other people's like the bluest of the "blues,"
So when "you're right there, Jerry lad," arises from the throng,
He'll croak: "Bedad ye may be right but - then ye may be wrong."

Mat Reilly is a socialist, Jim Byrne stands for peace,
But little Billy Hennessy has little time for these,
With five feet two drawn up to look like six he'll fiercely cry-
"Thank God, I'm still a Fenian, boys, and not afraid to die."

So though Westminster debates Home Rule for Erin still,
It has long passed the Parliament beside Knockallen hill;
Where destinies of nations, from Caesars down to George,
Are settled while a mare is shod in Jerry Connor's forge.

Patsy Maguire

Old Patsy Maguire lived down in Athlone,
He'd a neat little cottage and a field of his own,
His singing began with the first risen lark
And that same old "come all ye" would welcome the dark;
For only one song in the world did he know
And that was "a cháilin deas crúite na mbó."

His hair was as white and as thick as the frost
That lies on the meadows the pooka has crossed,
But the glint of his eye was as roguish and bright
As a daisy in May looking up to the light.
And the voice of him never a tremor did know
As he chanted "a cháilin deas crúite na mbó."

In the long winter nights there was never a fire
Could draw all the boys like the hearth of Maguire,
For he'd tell you of fairies and ghosts till your skin
Like a dead goose was puckered without and within,
And the road to your home was a horror beset
By all the dark 'spirits' that Patsy had met.

With the end of his stick in the ashes he'd show
How many a battle was fought long ago,
When his grandfather shouldered the pike that was laid
By the side of his bed with the notch on its blade.
"Sure some of them yeomen were tougher than wire
And steel couldn't stand them" said Patsy Maguire.

He had starved in the famine, the fever had known,
He had stood with the boys who struck out for their own;
He had dreamed with the dreamers, had met what they met,
"But failure's a word that we haven't spelt yet
And fighting's a game that all true men require
To keep them contented" said Patsy Maguire.

'Tis many a year since his footsteps were known
By the bridge and the river of storied Athlone,
And many a summer its riches has cast
O'er that sturdy old Fenian so true to the last;
But never a death chill could conquer the fire
That beat in the heart's blood of Patsy Maguire.

For far in those realms where brave men are blessed
And nothing's too good for earth's truest and best,
He is seated tonight in a place of his own
With a welcome for all from the town of Athlone;
And, whatever the songs of the seraphs, I know
He still sings "a cháilin deas crúite na mbó."

The racing of Finn McCool

'Twas Martin McDermott bought him from a man in the fair of Naas,
And never an uglier object was seen on a farmer's place;
He was lanky and long and bony, with a head like a tinker's mule,
And he had such a style of steppin' that we christened him Finn McCool.

But never a word said Martin, 'tis he is the knowing one!
He foddered the colt all winter and cantered him there and yon;
So a feather would knock me over when I heard that day in the town
That Finn McCool had been entered for the races of Punchestown.

Takin' a drop to brace me I started into Maynooth,
But twenty were there before me as anxious to know the truth;
And there sat deluderin' Martin, jokin' and playin' the fool,
Tellin' stories of this and that but nothin' of Finn McCool.

Tippin' a wink for myself to stay, he soon got rid of the lot
When the missus came out to call him to come while his tea was hot;
Of course a cup was there for myself and a plate full of pancakes brown,-
But what did I care for pancakes with my mind upon Punchestown!

Then Martin told me the pedigree of the grandsires both of Finn,
Though he was a base descendent of all of his famous kin;
"The horse has his points," said Martin, "though he runs like a circus clown,
But he stands to make me or break me at the races of Punchestown"

Don't talk of a month of waitin' till every cent you own
Is set on an ornary animal that's skin where he isn't bone;
I dreamed of him night and mornin' till my wife says, "Phlim O'Toole,
'Tis down in Carlow asylum you'll finish with Finn McCool."

At last the day of the races came; Martin, myself and the horse
With Davey Lacey to ride him, were early upon the course.
"How much against Finn McCool?" said I, and the bookie said with a grin,
"Twenty to one and the fun you'll have watchin' the others win."

Indeed I could never blame him when I saw the horses in line
Leap out like shots from a rifle when the starter flung up the sign,
And laggin' along behind them went Finn McCool at a pace
That would shame any decent donkey for sale at the fair in Naas.

"Go on ye devil," I yelled at him, "Go at it and lift your feet
Or by all the Fenians in Tir na nOg I'll shoot ye the day you're beat!"
And by me Martin McDermott was cursin' him dead and blind,
With the crowd all laughin' and shoutin' "arrah, look at the one behind!"

And he heard us, by all the gods of war! for he lepped like a frightened deer
And started off with Lacey, the jock, jig-sawin' from tail to ear;
Rearin' and tearin' and snortin' he clattered past horse by horse
While you'd think the end of the world had come by the roarin' upon the course.

With his big feet thrashin' like paddle wheels and his tail like a jury mast
He went over hurdle and double ditch till the first of the field was passed;
"He's winnin', he's winnin'," I heard, and then "take that" says I, "from O'Toole,"
As I flung my hat in the bookie's face who was laughin' at Finn McCool.

Winnin', of course he was winnin', with the people all goin' wild
And Martin McDermott crying beside me just like a child;
"Faith the omadaun doesn't know when to stop!"cried Kelly the vet from Clane,
For having near leaped through the judges box, Finn made for the hill again.

We followed him to the paddock where the horses were weighin' in,
And devil a hair was turned on the hide of that warrior, Finn;
As cool as his mighty namesake that never had known defeat
He seemed to be winkin' "a Fenian lad is a mighty hard thing to beat."

Well, the bookies paid us our money, and the crownin' joy of that race
Was countin' my bag of sovereigns from the lad I hit in the face;
"Be careful my boyo," says I to him, "next time when your cash goes down
That it isn't a Finn McCool you have, the winner of Punchestown".

A deoch an dorais

Here where my rhymes are ended
And you leave the old for the new
I'm pledging a deoch an dorais,
O, friends of my heart to you,
I know that my simple singing
Will fade from your ears as soon
As the song of a wayside robin
You heard by the road in June;
But the dreams I have dreamed for Ireland,
Please God they will never die
Till we're drinking a deoch an dorais
To the world itself, - Goodbye

A day with Pádraig Pearse

Never did a more beautiful day dawn on the city of Dublin – grey, old Dublin, sitting there by the Liffey, ever lovely, ever sad, ever hopeful – than that morning when I set out from my northside lodgings to spend a Sunday at St. Enda's, at the warm invitation of Pádraig Pearse. Some time before that I had met him in New York and he had told me about making a new record in scholastic affairs.

As I walked briskly down Rutland Square and past the Parnell monument my mind kept recurring to this young man, as I had known him in New York. What a wonderful personality he had! What a power to sway the crowds that flocked to hear his talks and lectures. "The white flame of a soul on fire," was how one writer described the impression he had created amongst those who had listened breathlessly to his address on Robert Emmet in one of the leading halls of that greater Ireland overseas.

Flower girls galore, in gaudy shawls and with the bright sunshine glinting on their braided hair – and, by the way, what wonderful hair most of these Dublin street hawkers have – besieged me with bouquets of every wild and garden flower known in Erin. "A penny a bunch lady, here, a penny a bunch. Do lady, buy a bunch to pin on that nice American dress you have. God knows I need the money with himself sick at home on me and the child here to be feedin'," appealed one of the most insistent pleaders.

Judging by appearance the "child here" was being fed all right, if red cheeks and dimpled chubby hands were any index. But there was no getting away from the sweet "deludher" of my own old town's tongue, more enticing ten times over, for all the years I had been away; so my pennies went like hotcross buns on a Good Friday.

By the time Nelson's Pillar was reached I was draped all over with cowslips and primroses while a cabbage leaf, filled with strawberries, was resting in my right hand and claiming instant attention. And that cabbage leaf got it, for nothing I know in berries comes near Irish strawberries for flavour and freshness.

But, alas, for being a glutton on berries! No sooner had I finished my last lucious fruit than about twenty insistent women were urging further cabbage leaves under my eyes: "She said tuppence, I'll make it a penny, ma'am. Just look at my strawberries – they're rale strawberries, fresh from the beds this mornin' and not out of the market like she buys them. Ma'am, here's rale strawberries at only a penny.

And then the unexpected happened. A rescuer from the far-off wild and glorious hills of Donegal hove into sight. Swinging down O'Connell Street came a man I had met in America two years before. A cigar was tilted at a dizzy angle between his lips and his nose and he was looking about him with that painful look of desire for something exciting to happen that an Irishman always wears in a quiet neighbourhood.

"Why, how do ye do," I cried, joyfully, "and how did you leave all the folks in Hoboken?"

The cigar fell to the sidewalk and my two hands were almost crushed in the vigorous clasp of my Ulster friend's sunburned fists.

"Well, well, and where did you come from yourself, and what are you doing here?"

When all the questions had been answered and he knew where I was going, my Ulster friend looked mighty sorrowful: "I wish I was going with you," he said, "a son of my old friend, McSweeny from Donegal, is there,"

"Why, then, come on," I said, "Pádraig Pearse will be glad to welcome an Irish speaker like you to his college. Anyhow, come on with me and meet one of the finest men that ever drew breath in a long time, and the man who is working as no man has ever worked before, at least since the days of Mangan and Davis, for a new Ireland.

And so, together, we boarded a Rathfarnham "tram" and started out to spend a day at St. Enda's College. Did you ever ride the top of a tram in June when the Dublin hills look their loveliest? If you haven't you have missed one of the sweetest experiences of your life. The soft, moist air strokes your face like a baby's fingers, as you are carried along, and a thousand and one sights and scenes, unknown to the foot passerby, are portrayed for your vision.

Little kitchen gardens, you will be seeing, hidden behind high ivy covered walls, backyards where riotous children "raise Cain" from morning to night, and for-lorn looking hens and chickens go clucking and scratching for juicy worms that never are to be found so close to a crowded city.

And then the heather-scent in your face, once you get outside of Dublin's smoke, with a hundred other beauties spreading themselves before you. Fields yellow with cowslips and buttercups, hedges decked with primroses, blue violets in the ditches and a glory of flowery hawthorn everywhere. Ireland in June, indeed, is surely a bit of heaven.

After leaving the tram there was yet about a mile to be travelled before we came to St. Enda's. It was a mile's walking to be remembered, with the pink and white confetti of hawthorn drifting over the road and larks and thrushes singing as only they sing in Ireland when summer is abroad.

And then we came to the big gates that guard St. Enda's College. A grey-eyed boy in Gaelic costume came forward to ask who we were and on what business we came. I told him all about it and he presented arms in a dignified salute and told us to "pass on."
We passed on. A wide, long avenue led us up to the grey old building, once a mansion belonging to a Dublin aristocrat – one of the "fine, ould stock" – and now dedicated to the greater purpose of educating Ireland's youth to Ireland's ideals. The big front door stood open, and, after hammering on its panels for a while, Pádraig himself stood before us.
"The white flame of a soul on fire"! How the saying surged back in my memory as I looked into those, wonderful eyes and saw the curves of that classic mouth and chin again. Surely, here was one who (to quote his own lines) never could "shun perilous deed or wrath, nor many mighty battles."

A "céad míle fáilte"as warm as the sunshine brooding over that glorious Dublin landscape, was given to myself and the man from Donegal who was with me, and maybe it wasn't a gay party that sat down together in that old, many windowed parlour of St. Enda's to chat awhile before lunch was served. It was out on the lawn we ate that lunch. It was right beside the tree set by Robert Emmet that I drank the most memorable cup of tea in all my existence, - and I have drunk many – and it was on the very spot where Emmet often came in his young days, to dream his dreams for Ireland, that I sat there picking at a chicken bone and thinking that, though Emmet's ashes were lying in an unknown tomb, his great successor was sitting before me, and that this was June 1914 and not 1803.

What the talk was all about I cannot tell you, for, you see, I do not know the old tongue of the Gael. My friend from Donegal and the other guest who sat that day at Pádraig Pearse's table thought I understood Irish and so included me in their conversation. Being an arrant coward I just nodded and smiled as if I knew, and mentally and spiritually kicked myself for having to be an outsider.

Anyhow, it sounded good to me and, though, to any woman, language that she cannot understand is always a maddening thing, this language was a joy to me for it was the language of my fathers, the tongue of the land that gave me birth, and it was my own fault altogether that I was unable to speak it.

When lunch was finished Pádraig Pearse told us he was due to deliver an address at a Volunteer meeting in Dundrum that afternoon and afterwards to speak at a feis in Dolphin's Barn. "A friend has sent his car to take me there," he explained, "and, if you do not object to a little crowding, I would be glad to have you accompany me."

Crowding! Why, to be "crowded" in with this wonderful "hero of the Gael," in life or death, would and could be nothing but an honour and a glory.

We piled into the waiting car and my latest vision of St. Enda's was of a noble old house with ivy clinging to it, here and there; roses, wild and cultivated, blooming on all sides, and a company of Fianna boys marching in military style across the smooth, green lawn. The boy who walked in front I shall never forget. He was a tall, straight-limbed youngster, bareheaded and in Irish kilt. His hair was flung off his forehead, the wind blew his cloak hither and thither, and I thought to myself: Surely, this is young Red Hugh O'Donnell, himself, come to life again. The boy was young MacSweeny, the son of that Donegal MacSweeny that my Ulster friend was so anxious to meet, and one of those imprisoned a year later for daring to be a pupil at St. Enda's.

As the car rolled on to Dundrum, Pádraig Pearse told us all about the history of the scenes we were travelling through: Here Robert Emmet walked with Sarah Curran; here the boys of '98 used to drill at night; here Thomas Davis and Richard Dalton Williams used to come for a walk on Sundays and talk about Ireland and "how does she stand."

All too soon we got to Dundrum and the Volunteer meeting. An immense crowd had assembled to hear Pádraig Pearse speak and when he stood on the platform you never heard such a thunder of applause as rose from that crowded park. Though short, his address was vibrant of the new soul that was stirring Ireland to life and action again, the soul that never again shall be baffled in its fight for freedom. He spoke for about half an hour, and then told the crowd, that was hanging on his every word, that he had to attend a feis in Dolphin's Barn.

Again we took the car and sped off between lines of cheering folks. I seem to see Pádraig Pearse now, as I saw him there that day, sitting, bare-headed, in the sunlight and with that shy, winning smile of his turned to the faces around him.

At Dolphin's Barn we stopped before the entrance to a little park where hundreds of people were gathered for the feis. A stage had been erected in a hollow, cup-shaped amphitheater and groups of men, women and children were sitting and standing in the surrounding hill slopes.

What a reception was given to Pádraig Pearse as soon as he was recognized!

He always seemed to shrink from applause, and, in his embarrassment, he stumbled on the rough steps leading to the stage and everyone laughed heartily when some voice called out, "You won't be married this year after that."

He spoke in Gaelic which he afterwards translated into English for those of us who did not understand their mother tongue. I think his pronunciation of Gaelic was the sweetest I have ever heard. Those hauntingly beautiful words fell from his lips like liquid silver, and he dwelt on every phrase as if it were – and it was – a joy for him to speak it.

After a very fine programme was concluded we were invited to have tea at a nearby house, and what a pleasant time we had there! There was everything one can imagine, with wheaten bread thrown in, on that table, and Pádraig Pearse laughed and joked and enjoyed himself like a schoolboy.

Several of those who had taken part in the feis were with us and we had another feis right there, in that cheery little parlour. A couple of delightful hours were passed with music and singing and dancing, one young fellow giving us a splendid selection of old Irish airs on the pipes.

The Dublin Hills were hidden under the shadows of night as we came back to the city. The last sleepy thrush had sung his final "goodnight" and cuddled down in his darkling nest as we rolled along the suburban air. Somehow, we were all strangely silent, like children who, though tired of play when darkness falls, are not yet ready for sleep. My Ulster friend spoke a few words, now and then, in Gaelic, and it seemed to be the only sound that was fitting to be heard there.

Again comes a vision of Pádraig Pearse seated beside me with his fine, and, I always thought, wistful, profile outlined against a yellow bar of sky where the sun had dropped out of sight but left that kindly trail of glory behind him which always illuminates a summer night in Ireland. We passed a group of boys and girls singing "A Nation Once Again"; evidently from some Gaelic meeting in the neighbourhood. A boy in Irish kilts was tuning a flute – a young Pan, without the horns, as he hurried along the road; a man was playing on a harp, outside of a "corner house", "The Wearin' of the Green".

The car sped on. Finally were in the city of Dublin again and in College Green. "They don't seem to be in a hurry about moving," I said, pointing over to the Bank of Ireland, once the Parliament House. Pádraig Pearse smiled. "It will take something more than the Bill of Home Rule to dislodge them, and they know it," he said.

When we came down to the Post Office, we parted. "When I come over to Ireland again," I said, "things will be different."

"Yes, they will be different," he said. Again he smiled that wonderful, shy, enigmatic smile of his. And so we clasped hands and said goodbye.

It is Easter Week in Ireland now again and "things are different."

Pádraig Pearse and those who died with him are lying in quick-limed graves, but their mission has been accomplished.

The soul of Ireland lives.

In the heart of the hills

"At the back of 'God Speed' entirely", we used to say it was long ago, when we were young and wanted to know and see more of the big world that lay the other side the hills. Now when we have had our desire and found that the edition of the village of Grange, many of us look back with "long, long thoughts" to it and all about it, over the seas and the years that lie between.

In the heart of the hills it lay, just a mile or two from the borders of Meath, that little County Kildare village of eleven houses, a Catholic Church, a graveyard and the local National School. Being a "commons", that is a waste piece of ground between boundaries, no one in Grange village had to pay rent except Miss Cully who lived in the "Big House" and owned several hundred acres of the surrounding land. The Church was built in the "hard times" often spoken of with bated breath by the old people, and had to hide itself down there where its spires might no offend the eyes of godly Protestant folks passing along the main roads of the country.

The "godly folks" never, perhaps, realized how much they missed, for that old Church, as well as being a gem in architecture, was the heart of a picture never to be forgotten framed there in the lap of the hills with big chestnut trees all around it and ten snug whitewashed cottages forming a circle about its gates, like a kind of loving bodyguard, to protect it from evil, day in and day out.

When the chestnut trees were in blossom in summer and the hawthorn hedges outside were sending whiffs of their perfume in through the open door and windows of that grey old Church where the little red lamp before the altar shimmed forever, no great Cathedral shrine in the big cities of the world could eclipse the peace and beauty to be found there. Sometimes an adventurous swallow would dart in on its airy flight and perch awhile near the altar and then I always thought of blessed Francis and his bird friends. In winter robins trooped in there all the time, and I know the loving sentinel behind the Tabernacle veil welcomed all His other children of a greater growth.

Outside and all around was the graveyard with oak, ash and elm trees shading it in, as if warding off the too joyous light of day from the sad little tombstones beneath; the "short and simple annals of the poor" there needed no searchlight from the sky to emblazon their virtues, very few folk coming to pray in "God's Acre" there but knew intimately the life story of all these sleepers.

Outside the iron railing surrounding the Church was the school . It was called the "national school" then when I learned my A B C there, but its only claim to nationality was that it had a national grant contributed , of course, from local taxpayers, and as a big concession, it also had the local parish priest as its director. But that director was as powerless to direct the policy of his school as a private in the trenches is to direct the firing of the corps behind him.

So our only "nationality" was derived from the teacher and from the Curate who used to come twice a week and teach us Thomas Davis' songs. When I first heard the tale of Fontenoy, I sat up all night by the light of a penny candle until I had mastered the whole story as told by Davis in his wonderful ballad. In the same way I mastered Michael Scanlan's ballad of "Jacket's Green" and several revolutionary recitations, which that same curate and his pastor handed on to us sub rosa so to speak.

These after hour's sessions were the most pleasant experiences of the week for us. Ten or twelve of the biggest pupils were selected for this literary class and there we were taught the history of our county behind closed doors. The national board of education in Ireland some years ago was the most anti-Irish institution in that much-tried country. Owing to the good work being done by the Gaelic League lately, however, Irish children have now a chance of becoming acquainted with the legends and poetry of their own land through their school books.

The school was a two storied dreary building and always felt chilly no matter how bright the sun shone outside. In winter it was a veritable icehouse when the wind screamed down the hills and rain lashed at the windows. The turf fire in a small grate at one end of the long room was never able to thaw out the shivering boys and girls who looked so longingly towards it. The fuel was generally donated by the parents of the wealthier scholars. The school board of course never thought of supplying such a luxury.

In the centre of Grange village was a square patch of ragged grass called "The Green". It was the happy hunting ground of a flock of bedraggled hens that scratched and clucked there all day and fought over the chunks of bread thrown away by the school children. In the long hungry days of March some of the more desperate of these feathered pirates have actually come up the school stairs and attacked the children's lunch baskets. Those Grange hens could surely be trusted to scratch out their living.

There was one shop in Grange. It's whole stock in trade was contained in one window and consisted of candies, starch, blue, soap, sugar, tea, and a lot of little odds and ends. Candies, however, were most in demand and the small person who had a penny to spend at "Anne's" for barley sugar or bull's eyes was ever the most popular and envied one in school.

Opposite the church gate lived a little dressmaker who made a scanty living sewing for the old fashioned folks around who didn't need their garments patterned after the latest Paris style. Catherine did not believe in sewing machines and would not touch one with a forty-foot pole. She believed in strong thread and good sewing and certainly her work would hardly be ripped asunder. She always had a mug of fresh water or buttermilk for a thirsty child, and her clean cozy fireside was a welcome haven for certain privileged favourites during playhour on rainydays.

One of the eleven houses had two stories and must have been a fine residence at one time. It had rose bushes and apple trees in the garden, but, after the original owner died, it passed from one tenant to another, getting shabbier year by year, like some poor old derelict whom no one cares for any more.

Miss Cully's house was the show place of the village. The big garden was a delightful place, brilliant in summer with tulips and hollyhocks. Magnificent chestnut trees shaded the old avenue along whose banks the first primroses and violets were to be found in spring.

A dear, drowsy, peaceful village was Grange, snuggled down among the hills and overlooked from the distance by the blue mountains of Wicklow. When I saw it last year, though, what a change was there! only six houses were standing still, with the church and school. Anne the shopkeeper, Catherine the dressmaker, old Kitty, who could still dance an Irish jig at eighty, Miss Cully – all were gone. The very hens seemed to be of a different breed and walked around in a prim sedate manner quite different to the aggressive old warriors of old that burrowed on "The Green".

The only thing unchanged in the little village was the church the graveyard and the school. His British Majesty had awarded a glaring red letterbox, and the county council board had erected a pump in Grange, but indeed Grange, with its dozen of a population, has little use for either.

But the air is still very sweet there and the hills around as tenderly green as ever. Altogether, when the chestnut trees are in blossom and the hawthorn bushes all white it is a pleasant place to visit, that old village of Grange, even if it is "at the back of God speed entirely".

Daffodils

"Was that Mrs. Dugan I saw coming out of here just now with an armful of flowers?" I asked Ellen Molloy, who was in a perfect frenzy of work in her cluttered apartment, where every article of furniture was draped with odds and ends of feminine wear in all stages of manufacture.

Ellen took her time answering, which was natural enough, seeing that her mouth was filled with pins and that she was making cabalistic signs on a scrap of wrapping paper with a stub of a pencil. She nodded assent, however, and soon cleared her oral cavity of its burden much to my relief, who always feared an inadvertent sneeze on her part on such occasions.

"Ay, that was Mrs. Dugan," she said. "And it's a good thing her coat is nearly finished, for she has me in a frazzle about it. Every day she's in here with some new idea in her head about this or that, as if I could change a thing after it's cut out and half put together. Day before yesterday she wanted pockets and then thought they might stick out too much and spoil the lines of her figure. 'Spoil the lines of a feather bed!' says I to myself and I tryin' to be polite to her. Then she thought a belt would be sort of stylish till I talked her out of it. Anybody who would put a belt on Mrs. Dugan should either be sent to jail or

Grangegorman, for a waist is one thing she hasn't got. However, I ended all discussions this mornin'; and promised to have her coat all ready by tomorrow, when I'll be able to get to some of my other work."

I gave a quick glance round the room to see if there were any signs of my own modest garment being nearer Ellen's ministrations than it had been a week ago. Alas! there it was still hanging in dejected privacy behind the door, a forlorn object, a mere ghost of a garment – sleeveless, hemless, formless. I said nothing, but I looked Ellen sadly in the eyes. She did not quail before that mute reproach.

"I know what you're thinkin', she said airily, but I'll put that dress of yours together in the mornin' please God, as quick as a cat would be lickin' her ear. Sure, what makin' does there be on the like of a thing like that? A few seams to run up, a couple of sleeves to put in, and there you are. Seein' you're as thin as a herrin' I won't have to be pastin' you down or pullin' you in; but with a coat for a fat woman like Mrs. Dugan it's different." Here Ellen launched out into the troubles of her profession while I listened in silence, knowing that the harder she talked the harder she worked, and that every lick put into Mrs. Dugan's coat brought Ellen nearer to my own shapeless garment behind the door.

"What was she doin' with the armful of daffodils?" I asked at length when I could get a word in edgeways with Ellen, my mind still being full of Mrs. Dugan and the lovely spring blooms she was carrying so proudly along the sidewalk.

Ellen gave me a long look. "You're a queer woman," she said. "Here you're livin' in Drumcondra for more years that there are pins on the floor and you come askin' me for information about your neighbours! You see Mrs. Dugan nearly every day goin' to the chapel or doin' her marketin' even if you don't know her friend, Mrs. Kelly, yet you have to come to a busy woman like me for information about her and her annual flower festival as I call it." I looked at the countless pins on the floor, and though my blood boiled at Ellen's reckoning I still kept silent, for when she has a story to tell interruptions are not in order. She now pointed to a chair with a back — which probably accounted for its not being draped with something wearable — and said if I'd be taking the basting threads out of Rose Reilly's new dress which she had just finished she would tell me all I wished to know about Mrs. Dugan and her armful of daffodils. "And you'd better be careful of that dress," she said "for the seams are narrow and the stuff so thin a hard pull will destroy it on me entirely." I promised to handle Rose's gown with tender hands, for she is a hefty girl and needs her seams to have their full power of resistance left intact.

"It's many a long day since Bride Kearney, Mrs. Dugan's sister and myself served our time together in Madame Devanne's warerooms here in Dublin," thus Ellen began her recital. Madame was just plain Margaret Devanney in private life, and a fine big woman she was sweepin' along in her silk dresses with a gold watch stuck on the front of her like a Town Hall clock. From Roscommon she came before she put the French twist to her name, but she knew her business and would talk down to the best of them who used to come in their carriages to her rooms. That was the time when clothes weren't turned out of a factory like chairs and tables the way they are now, neither did women try to copy Paris models from a sixpenny pattern out of Woolworth's. No! indeed, if the League of Nations put as much plannin' and work into its job today as we used to put into one costume at Madame Devanne's long ago there would be no more wars. But it was a hard and slavish life, and the few shillings we were paid when we came to the time of earnin' would hardly buy a pair of stockings now. Of course dressmakin' is a thing of the past, for few come to us now except the ones neither factory nor pattern can fit like yourself and Mrs. Dugan and others who are either as flat as a tram track or so bunchy that no rule holds good with them.

Here I shot another indignant glance at Ellen, but she took no notice of me, being deeply absorbed in the set of Mrs. Dugan's sleeve. Presently she continued:

The Kearney's came from somewhere in Wicklow, and Rose would be tellin' me how the daffodils about this time of year would be yellow as gold in their garden. It was like seein' them to be hearin' her, and we with nothin' before our eyes but dirty windows and the smokey sky above George's Street here in Dublin. The poor creature is dead many a year ago and lyin' in Wicklow now with the daffodils blowin' above her. By the time Madame considered us worth our first five shillings a week wages Bride was due for the long rest that comes to us all some time. God be good to her this day, Amen!

But to be getting' on with my story. On account of knowin' poor Bride so well her sister Mary often came to see me when she married Tom Dugan, a conductor on the Donnybrook tram, and settled here in the city. I never took to her somehow, like I did to Bride, for she was a different sort of person altogether, but when I started business for myself in one room she often threw a bit of trade in my way, and, of course, gave me her own clothes to make, for she was no earthly good at a needle herself. Mrs. Dugan also liked to tell about her 'dressmaker' anyway; she is like that, you know.

Many a time I'd be told about what her friend Mrs. Kelly, would be doin' and sayin', always with the additional information that Mr. Kelly held 'a position' in the Custom House – for 'a position', as you know beats a plain 'job' off the map. Naturally I was delighted when Mrs. Dugan brought her friend one day to be measured for a new dress. I thought this Mrs. Kelly was a nice, quite sort of woman, but, except for the reflected glory of her husband's white collar 'position' not such a shinin' light as I had imagined her to be. Well, anyway, I made the dress for her and she paid me, though I may as well tell you she thought it was longer in the back than in the front, and wanted to know if there was any of the material left over in case she had to patch it later on. Here I couldn't help snorting a little, for it is not Ellen Molloy's weakness to skimp on stuff, and then hand you back a piece of your material that is no good for anything but future patches. "Don't sneeze over that dress," she said; "Rose Reilly will be as fussy as a wet hen if she sees a spot on it." I meekly denied wanting to sneeze, so Ellen continued:-

I only saw this Mrs. Kelly once after that, though I still kept hearin' about her and the important people that Mrs. Dugan met through their acquaintance. She gave me no more work, but one day when I asked about her Mrs. Dugan says, 'Oh Mrs. Kelly is havin' her things made now by a tailoress in Henry Street, but I believe in stickin' by old friends, and you suit me all right, Miss Molloy. Just think of havin' that remark handed to you when I was makin' her clothes for less than she'd get them done anywhere, just for poor Bride's sake. Don't be talkin', but some of the people a body has to contend with in business should be kept under lock and key for the good of the public.

Well, one Sunday afternoon some years ago I was takin' a walk through the Park, plannin' over the week's work ahead of me and wonderin' how I could get some money due to me out of a couple of hard cases who would hold on to a shillin' till their nails split when who should I see comin' out of the Zoo gate but Mrs. Kelly and another woman, all dressed up in their best and wantin' everyone to take notice of it. I bowed to Mrs. Kelly, but whether she saw me or not she ignored the salute, and went off chatterin' about how sorry she was Captain Rigney wasn't there to enjoy the day with them.

Now, anyone may meet anyone else in the Park on a Sunday, but what set me thinkin' was why Mrs. Kelly should be paradin' around without her bosom friend, as Mrs. Dugan often told me they always spent their Sunday afternoons together either out walkin' or visitin' the pictures. Of course it was none of my business, but you know how a thing will stay in you mind sometimes; so when Mrs. Dugan dropped in here the next day I said I was glad to see she wasn't sick or anything as I noticed she wasn't havin' her usual walk with Mrs. Kelly the day before.

Woman dear, but I put my foot in it! "What do you mean about Mrs. Kelly been' in the Park?" I was asked. "Mrs. Kelly and her husband were visiting in the country all day yesterday, so I stayed at home, not being one to go paradin' around by myself like a lost sheep. You must be losin' your eyesight, Miss Molloy, to make such a mistake."

I had made no mistake, and I told her so then plain enough, describin' Mrs. Kelly's new hat and dress and how the one with her had one of these spectacles stuck on a handle that she held on her nose every now and then. "They were talkin about a Captain Rigney," says I. "Mrs. Kelly was so sorry he wasn't there with them to enjoy the day."

Well, my dear, a silence fell on this room so complete that I heard a child cryin' two houses away. Mrs. Dugan just said perhaps her friend had changed her mind about goin' to the country, and off she went without sayin' another word, good, bad, or indifferent. Of course, as I said before, it was none of my business, but I felt sorry that I had let some cat out of its bag.

My dear, it wasn't a cat I let out of a bag at all, but a tiger, as you will hear. Rose Reilly told me all about it one day soon after, the same Rose being one who knows more that the daily papers are able to publish. You know Rose lives next door to the Kellys, so as she heard a great commotion in their back parlour one mornin' she stationed herself where she could get the benefit of the loud talk. It was Mrs. Dugan freein' her mind of all she thought about her old-time friend goin' off walkin' with Mrs. Rigney in the Park, after tellin' her she would be in the country that day. It appears the Rigneys were people that Mrs. Dugan had been dyin' to meet, but so far had been kept in the background whenever they were around. Rose said the way she carried on was something to remember, and the worst of it was that Mrs. Kelly made no apology at all about the whole business more than sayin' she was tied to nobody and would go walkin' with anyone she liked independent of what her other friends thought about it. For an hour they kept at it, hammer and tongs, till Rose heard Kelly's front door bang shut and silence fell on the scene again.

Needless to say, Mrs. Kelly's name was never mentioned when Mrs. Dugan came in here after that, and it was Rose Reilly who kept me posted as to the rest of the happenings between them. About six months after the big doings Tom Dugan's uncle died down the country somewhere and left him his little place. Not wantin' to take up farmin' in these hard times, and as he was more use to runnin' a tram than handlin' a plough, Tom sold out the whole concern, and the first thing himself and Mary decided to do was to buy a house where the children would have more advantages than in rented quarters. Young ones today want all the style they can get, and I don't blame the Dugans for gettin' a place to themselves where they can live in peace and decency. So they got a nice new house with a bathroom and all the fixings in a row that the builders were just after finishing. Herself asked me to come and see them when they were settled, but, to tell the truth, I have no time to go visitin' and by all I hear people sayin' about their callers I think it's safer to stay at home sometimes and keep out of trouble.

Well, to be getting' on with my story; It seems that the Dugans were livin' on top of the world, and herself had only one wish, and that was she should get nice neighbours about her, as the houses were fillin' up very quickly. On the same day both houses beside were taken – one by a young married couple who were rentin' part of it, and the other by – who do you think?''

"By the Kellys," said I, nearly dropping Rose Reilly's precious dress on the floor.

"You're right," laughed Ellen; "by the Kellys''. Mrs. Dugan was out somewhere when the furniture was moved in next door and knew nothing till she went out in her yard to take some things off the line after comin' home, and there across the fence was Mrs. Kelly in her yard sweepin' a piece of carpet. Woman dear, it must have been a great sight to see the two of them glarin' at each other like a pair of cats, not knowin' which should strike first. I'd rather have seen it than the best show in Dublin.

"Which of them got in the first lick?" I asked breathlessly.

Ellen shook her head. "There were no blows," she answered. It was too big a shock to both of them. But then and there started a bloodless warfare that seldom had an equal. If either of them hung out her washing the other started to riddle ashes or sweep rugs, week after week, till both back yards were in a kind of siege. The Dugans played their gramophone till all hours of night, having moved it against the wall where the Kellys would have full benefit of the performance, and the Kellys made sure their wireless would be in full cry whenever they knew that the Dugans wanted silence – for Tom Dugan had to get sleep when he could, being mostly on late work. And so it was war to the knife and no quarter given for nearly a whole year.

And then, whether it was her nerves gave way or she got cold standin' guard by her washin' on a cold day in the yard, Mrs. Dugan fell sick. Pneumonia it was, and for a couple of weeks little hope was held for her recovery. And for all that time not a bit of ashes was riddled next door or a carpet beaten, and the wireless got a well-deserved rest. Poor Mrs. Dugan was out of her head completely, and all the time kept ravin' about her old home in Wicklow and the garden full of daffodils. She wanted some of the daffodils, and cried for them night and day.

"And then what do you suppose happened"? One day in marched Mrs. Kelly with an armful of bright yellow daffodils and straight up to where Mrs. Dugan was lyin' in her bed, and put the flowers down beside her. 'Here you are, Mary," says she. "I went down to Wicklow this mornin' and got these out of your old garden for you." And with that she kissed her, while everyone in the room looked as if the end of the world was comin' on top of them. Mrs. Dugan grabbed up the flowers and hugged them like they were a new baby, and – would you believe me? – in ten minutes she was fast asleep. Talk of cures – did you ever hear a quicker one then that?

Mrs. Kelly did more than that. "You're all tired out," says she to the family in the room; "go and take your rest and I'll stay here by Mary for the rest of the day." Which she did, and for other days, too, till peace was roostin' in both houses and the last gun silenced.

So there's my story now, and I only have to add that every year since on the anniversary of the armistice between the two families Mrs. Dugan presents her neighbour with the finest armful of daffodils she can buy in Dublin. Next Sunday she is goin' off for the day's outin' with the Kelly's and Rigneys, and that is when this coat is first to be flashed on an admiring public. "How about that dress of Rose Reilly's?" "Are you sure you got out all those bastin' threads without makin' a hole or puckerin' the material? If you did either, I'll be havin' another war to chronicle when you come for your fittin' next Tuesday."

"Oh, Ellen, will it be ready for tryin' on so soon?" I asked with hope for the neglected garment behind the door stirring in my heart.

Ellen sniffed. "Sure I could drape it in a broom handle and it would be a fit for you," she said disdainfully. "What makin' is there on a thing like that? No matter what you do, it will look two yards of pump water. But when it comes to makin' a coat – especially a coat for a fat woman like Mrs. Dugan – that's where a skilled hand is needed."

Newtown